Just me and the kids

A manual for lone parents

Just me and the kids

A manual for lone parents

**Developed by Gingerbread and the
Community Education Development Centre**

Published by Bedford Square Press in association with Gingerbread
and the
Community Education Development Centre

Published by
BEDFORD SQUARE PRESS
of the
National Council for Voluntary Organisations
26 Bedford Square, London WC1B 3HU
in association with

GINGERBREAD
35 Wellington Street, London WC2E 7BN
and the

COMMUNITY EDUCATION DEVELOPMENT CENTRE
Lyng Hall, Blackberry Lane, Coventry CV2 3JS

First published 1990
© Gingerbread 1990

Printed and bound in Great Britain by
J W Arrowsmith Limited, Bristol

Designed and produced by the
Community Education Development Centre, Coventry

British Library Cataloguing in Publication Data
Just me and the kids: a manual for lone parents.
    (Survival handbooks).
    1. Great Britain. Single-parent families
    I. Title II. Series
    362.82940941

ISBN 0-7199-1266-0

Contents

Contributors

We cannot acknowledge here all of the lone parents, Gingerbread groups, advisors and workers who have made a contribution to this project. We hope that you will each recognise how your experiences and suggestions have helped to shape this book. The people listed below are those who had a specific part to play in putting the book together.

Project Advisory Group
Annette Arthur, Doug Bollen, Diane Bond, Ann Brayshaw, Ashra Burman, Elaine Burrell, Janet Carlton, Anne Clarke, Sue Commons, Naomi Eisenstadt, Sue Emerson, Shirley Gounder, Pam Hill, Karon Jack, Sabera Jaffer, Andrew Jamieson, Fleur Jeremiah, Hetta Lucas, Rosemary McGregor, Ros Patchett, Ann Phoenix, Pat Ramsahye, Lee Sheridan, Lesley Smith, Judy Warner, Tina Wiseman

Critical readers
Ashra Burman (Community worker and freelance trainer), Jonathan Croall (Bedford Square Press), Naomi Eisenstadt (Save the Children), Julie Kaufmann (BBC Children in Need), Ann Phoenix (Thomas Coram Research Unit), Maggi Smith

Project Management Committee
Berwyn Peet (Gingerbread), Robbi Robson (Gingerbread), John Rennie (Community Education Development Centre)

Learning Together Project Team
Leila Carlyle, Berwyn Peet (Gingerbread) Martin Flynn, Ronny Flynn, Brian Sayer, Carolyn Sugden (Community Education Development Centre)

Design and production
Christine Knight, Bipun Tugnait, Sandra Wilson

Publication
Jonathan Croall, Carole Fries, Marianne Harper, Lynne Jarché

Project Manager
Brian Sayer

The Project Team fully acknowledges the influence of other writers and researchers in this field, many of whose materials were used to trigger discussions and recollections in the early stages of the project. Specific acknowledgement is given to the influence of: Hilary Graham, whose article 'Being poor: perceptions and coping strategies of lone mothers' was published in *Give and take in families* edited by Julia Brannen and Gail Wilson (published by Allen and Unwin in 1987); Carol Murdock, who wrote *Single parents are people too* (Butterick, 1980); and Jacqueline Burgoyne who wrote *Divorce matters* with Roger Ormrod and Martin Richards (Penguin, 1987).

We would like to thank the National Council for One Parent Families, for giving us access to their library and research files.

This project was undertaken with a special grant from the Department of Health, to whom we would like to express our gratitude.

Gingerbread is the leading support organisation in Britain for all lone parents and their children. It is a registered charity, run and managed by lone parents themselves, and responds to the changing needs of one parent families by providing local and national services to help them improve the quality of their lives. For further details, or information about local groups, contact Gingerbread, 35 Wellington Street, London WC2E 7BN Telephone 071 240 0953.

About this book

We wanted *Just me and the kids* to be written by experts, so we called on lone parents all over the country to provide the ideas, the framework and the first-hand stories.

Hundreds of lone parents all over Britain were involved in writing this book. The 'Learning together' project was set up by Gingerbread and the Community Education Development Centre in November 1988. The project team consulted lone parents throughout the country, sending out questionnaires, running meetings, visiting lone parent groups and talking with individual lone parents. Many people sent in accounts of their days, how they coped with difficulties, their children's feelings, their hopes and plans for the future.

Lone parents were asked what they thought were the most important issues.

The project team then produced a version of the book which was thoroughly read and tested by lone parents who tried out the exercises, wrote new accounts and commented on what we had written. Another couple of hundred people tried out some of the exercises from the book in Gingerbread group meetings, and in workshops at Gingerbread's 1989 AGM and holiday week.

The revised version was then sent out to a panel of readers, each of whom was a specialist in some aspect of parenting or childcare. They carefully assessed the style and content, and looked at the messages conveyed in the book. A final version was then written to take their suggestions into account.

The result, you will agree, is a readable, helpful, positive guide to lone parenting which reflects a very wide range of real people's experiences.

Just me and the kids

This is a book by, for and about lone parents. It starts off by looking at the benefits of being alone and all the way through it emphasises the positive aspects of lone parenting. However, it does not avoid the fact that lone parents can face problems bringing up their children. This book will not give you instant solutions, but it will help you to think about your situation and work towards changing what you can, accepting what you cannot change and making the most of what you already have.

There are a million lone parents in Britain today, looking after more than one and a half million children. One parent families make up about one in seven of all families.

The one parent family is not a new phenomenon. Lone parents have been here for a long time and will continue to be part of society, represented in all ethnic and age groups, classes and lifestyles. The 'pen portraits' on the next two pages, by just a few of the parents who were involved in writing this book, show that there is no such thing as a 'typical' lone parent.

Lone parents *do* face problems, mainly because our society is built around the idea that it is normal for two people to share in bringing up their children, and for one of the parents to look after the children while the other goes out to earn the money.

Lone parents have to do both these jobs, whilst living in a society that assumes that the roles will be split. It is not surprising that lone parents are usually financially worse off than other parents. The support that they need is not always available — whether it is childcare, training opportunities, emotional support or job opportunities.

Just me and the kids should be helpful to any lone parent because:

- it starts from the viewpoint that a one parent family is a normal family unit
- it places importance on your experience and the experiences of other lone parents
- it recognises that lone parents want to improve their situations, make changes and look to the future.

The book contains questionnaires, exercises, case studies and accounts written by lone parents which will help you reflect on your own situation. It is a book to make you feel good about being a lone parent and to help you grow stronger and more confident.

Who is the book for?

We have tried to make *Just me and the kids* interesting and useful to all lone parents. Lone fathers as well as mothers, teenagers, widowed people, black people, lesbian and gay lone parents, those who work outside the home and those who do not, disabled lone parents — all have been involved in writing the book and all have a place in it.

No book can cater for everyone's needs at once. Some chapters will be of more immediate interest to divorced or separated lone parents, and widowed lone parents or women who have chosen to have children alone will find these chapters do not have so much to say to them. The chapters on stress and managing your time will also have more relevance to some lone parents than to others. But, on the whole, we think you will find plenty of interest, whoever you are.

We hope that *Just me and the kids* will give you new ideas and a fresh outlook on parenting alone, summarised by one of the people who read the final version:

'Any lone parent reading this manual will find situations, experiences and feelings with which they are immediately familiar. They will find reassurance that their own reactions and solutions are appropriate and of value. They will gain many new insights into their own strengths, and a wealth of new ideas and suggestions on how to tackle some of the most difficult areas of life as a parent bringing up young children alone.'

If this book has one message in particular, it must be that it is not 'just you and the kids'. There are many other people who have had to face the same challenges as you, and you can benefit and learn from their experiences. You will find some of these experiences on the pages of this book. You will find many more if you can make contact with other lone parents and offer your support and friendship.

Just us and the kids

Linda

Linda has been a lone parent for six years. She has two children, aged 10 and 8. The youngest lives with her.

'I don't see myself as a "lone parent". I see myself as living on my own with a child, and sharing parenting with my children's father who lives elsewhere. I have a wide group of friends. I became a lesbian four years ago, and would like to have another child.'

Roy

'I am about 50 years old and I have been married twice. My first wife died leaving me with seven young children to bring up. I became disabled after being in a car accident whilst I was married to my first wife. I have also been in and out of hospital during the last couple of years for tests and major surgery. I had two children by my second marriage which ended due to adultery on my wife's part.'

Pat

Pat's husband died six months ago. She has one daughter aged 24 and another aged 7. She works as a childminder and a freelance childcare tutor.

'I really don't know the "new me" yet. I have been devastated by the loss of my husband — we were like one person in two bodies. Now I must seek a new life which I did not choose or want. It's an uphill struggle but — I shall survive!'

Sunita

Sunita has been a lone parent for seven years. She has one son aged 15 and works as a community development worker in the social services department of a shire county.

'I am 37 years of age, of Asian origin (Hindu Punjabi), born in India. Since becoming a lone parent I have qualified as a lecturer in further education, and I now enjoy working in a professional capacity. I have written a vegetarian Indian cookery book — I am a vegan, and I believe in a collective style of living, as I live in a housing collective. I am quite politically active and I consider myself to be a feminist.'

Donatella

'I have been a lone parent for eight years. I am 29 years old and mother of four children, all aged under 10. I am a state enrolled nurse and a secretary, but I've also worked as a cleaner and a childminder. At the moment I'm unemployed. Hopefully I'll soon be a degree student. My children are of mixed race. I live on state benefits. My home belongs to the local council.'

Sayadah

Sayadah has always been a lone parent. She works as a training officer for a childcare charity.

'I'm a black women in my mid-thirties with one child aged 3. I lead a very busy life, working full-time and sharing the care of my child with his father. I am fairly well organised, have a wide circle of mainly women friends, enjoy going out with them, inviting friends around. Most of my friends have children, though some have older children than mine.'

Trevor

Trevor has been a lone parent for nearly three years. His children are aged 4 and 7.

'I am a 40 year old man with two young girls. I work as a carpenter five days a week, from 7.30 to 5.00. Weekends I try to go out with the children to places like the zoo, but it normally ends up with us doing shopping and errands together.'

Frank

'My partner and I split up six months ago. I had always cared for my daughter so it seemed natural for me to carry on. But my employers were not sympathetic to me being a lone parent so I've decided to change my career and will soon be training to be a social worker. My daughter is now 18 months old.'

Maddie

'I became a single parent the day my first son was born, shortly after my sixteenth birthday. It was frightening to say the least. I felt helpless with this tiny creature, plus I suffered from baby blues and did not bond with him until he suffered severe asthma, when instinct, love and emotion finally came to the surface. Two years later I got pregnant again by accident, and support from strong friends helped me when the father decided he didn't want to know.'

Jan

'I'm 26 and have been sharing a house with another single parent for the past two years. This has its ups and downs, but on the whole works well. At the moment I'm very involved with working for my lone parents' group but have been taking 'O' levels and am about to take some 'A' levels with a view to being better qualified for a better job in the future.'

1 On our own — and doing fine

'The feeling of not being bossed around. More time with the children. The power of having my own money. The confidence to go out with no feelings of guilt; to push myself forward in every way.'

'No rows over children. Eat what and when I like. Go out where and with whom I choose. Fall asleep on the settee without being nagged. Watch what I like on television.'

This chapter highlights some of the positive aspects of lone parenting. Lone parents themselves know what is good about bringing up children alone, but other people may not see advantages, only problems. Sometimes, influenced by these people, lone parents may begin to doubt their own experiences. Sometimes they may feel so overwhelmed by day-to-day pressures that they cannot see any benefits.

The checklist on this page shows what the lone parents who took part in writing this book felt were the best aspects of lone parenting. As you read through the list, tick any that apply to you. At times when you feel down, use the list to remind you of the good sides of parenting alone.

All of the statements are about personal qualities and their development. Women, in particular, had gained a great deal from being lone parents. Time and time again they mentioned how they were able to find out who they were, instead of just being someone's wife or partner.

'I have become an individual again, not someone's wife. I have realised that my needs do matter and I should be able to enjoy life.'

'I have discovered great reserves of strength and willpower within myself. I have achieved more in five years than in all the other years put together.'

'You do not know what you can do until you try.'

Some people had gained new insights on families:

'I know that being two (parent and child) is being a family.'

'I now believe fathers can bring up children alone.'

Many lone parents had found that being alone was good for the whole family; the children were happier and doing better at school; the family was secure.

'I know that whatever we have got now is ours and no one can take it from us.'

'You do not have to be bitter. If access is worked out properly, the children can benefit more from having a part-time father who shows interest than from having a full-time one who cannot cope. It's given them and me more independence and we all let go of each other, which has enhanced our relationships.'

Strengths of being alone

- ❑ I have become independent.
- ❑ I have grown stronger.
- ❑ I have become more confident.
- ❑ I have developed new skills and hobbies.
- ❑ I am now able to stand up for myself.

- ❑ I can do things I did not think possible.
- ❑ I have taken stock and sorted out my life.
- ❑ I have made relationships.
- ❑ I can be myself, a person in my own right.
- ❑ I can survive on my own.

- ❑ I am free to make my own decisions.
- ❑ I can plan for the future by myself.
- ❑ I can be a good parent.
- ❑ I can give support to other people
- ❑ I am in control of my future.

- ❑ I have become aware that I am intelligent.
- ❑ I know that I am better off than some.
- ❑ I am able to make my own money decisions.
- ❑ My children and I are happier.
- ❑ I am closer to the children.

- ❑ I like myself; I am proud of myself.
- ❑ I know families do not always need two parents.

We asked four people to write about their positive experiences of being lone parents (none of them had felt positive about being on their own at the beginning). As you read through the accounts, look out for the strengths that these parents have developed.

Martin

'I hadn't taken much responsibility for my children. I suppose I was very traditional as a father. I went out to work, and only saw the children for an hour a day, at weekends and during the holidays. I didn't really know them at all. So when my wife left us suddenly, it was a disaster. We didn't have any family nearby, so I was forced to take responsibility for the children, or bring in outside help. The children were really unsettled, so I took all my holiday at once and the firm gave me an extra two weeks' unpaid leave. In those six weeks I got to know my children. We talked together, grieved together and became close. I kept up their school, playgroup and friends. I bought books on home management and got on with learning how to run a house.

'Looking back, I am so glad I stayed with the children. I now know that I was a father only in name. I have found feelings I didn't know I had. I've learned how to be caring and patient, gentle and kind. It hasn't been easy and I've faced a lot of prejudice from my male work colleagues who seem to think I should find another woman as soon as possible to take my wife's place.'

Diane

'I had to get out of my marriage in the end — he had started knocking the children about as well as me. I lost my home, my job and my family all in one week when I left. I went to stay with a friend 200 miles away. She put me in touch with a refuge where I got advice. But I felt safe for the first time in seven years. I knew then I had to make a new life, and I haven't looked back.

'What we have now has been built up by us alone. It's been really hard work but I'm independent, have some very close friends and a job I like. I would never have believed it.'

Marsha

'I had a long-term relationship with another woman, and we decided to have a child by artificial insemination. But before Sacha was born my partner ended it and I became a lone parent. I had a very difficult six months; the people at work were great but I hated the evenings alone, feeling tired and stuck in the flat. Most of my friends didn't have children. I decided I had to change where I lived and my whole way of life. I didn't want to be isolated and have the total responsibility for a home and children. So I looked in magazines and also advertised for a women's house needing new members. Sacha and I visited three and stayed the weekend before we found one that felt comfortable, and where we fitted in as well. If I hadn't become a lone parent I'd never have tried a new way of living — it's so much more supportive.'

Barbara

'My husband died a year ago and his death threw me into a different world, where I was unprotected from so much. It made me realise how much I'd left to him to do — all the finance, the garden, the car, all the practical things around the home. Taking it all on became a challenge, showing that I could do it. Sometimes I cried with frustration, there was so much to learn. But my daughter was marvellous and she never lost confidence in me. One year later, I now feel in control of my surroundings. I have enough money to pay for things I cannot or do not want to do myself — I went back to working full-time six months ago — and I've applied to train as a social worker. I still miss him but I have found strengths I never knew I had.'

2 Parenting alone

'I've learned independence and to think positively. If I want to do something, I find out about ways of achieving it and I go ahead and do it without being afraid of the outcome.'

'I've learned problem solving, financial juggling acts and numerous things like fixing bikes, decorating, cutting hair, and repairs of all descriptions.'

'I find it difficult to compliment myself and see the skills I have.'

Raising children requires many different skills. These are shared when two parents live together, but a lone parent has to learn to do everything without the support of a partner.

This chapter looks at the complex job which lone parents have to manage — and how they do it.

Twenty-five lone parents, when asked about the abilities, challenges and skills involved in lone parenting, came up with this list.

Lone parents become:
- able to manage changes
- good at managing money
- independent
- responsible
- well-organised
- able to cope
- close to their children
- good at making decisions.

Lone parents often face:
- prejudice and discrimination
- unwanted sexual advances
- battles with health and social services
- greater demands if their child is disabled
- making major decisions alone
- having no time off
- being seen as 'not real men'
- being seen as failures at relationships.

Lone parenting involves:
- having a sense of humour
- sharing
- having fun
- working hard
- fighting for what we believe in
- caring
- women gaining control over their lives
- seeing things through to the end.

Difficult situations

We asked lone parents to give us examples of situations where they had to learn to do things by themselves. Read through this list, on your own or with a friend. Which situations are familiar to you?

- ❏ Practical situations: when I need to change a plug, change a broken window pane, sewing and mending.
- ❏ Coping when I am not at my best — through illness, disability, etc.
- ❏ Coping when the children are ill.
- ❏ Not having enough money.
- ❏ Dealing with loneliness and isolation.
- ❏ Missing adult company, especially at night.
- ❏ Having to do everything for myself and the children and making all the decisions all the time.
- ❏ Finding someone trustworthy to look after the children.
- ❏ Not having someone else emotionally involved with the children to discuss day-to-day problems with.
- ❏ Having to discipline the kids alone and coping with them when they are being difficult.
- ❏ Coping with full-time work and childcare.
- ❏ Difficulties with housing and being made homeless.

Most of the lone parents had looked on these situations as a challenge, and worked to develop the skills they needed.

Money management

Having a child alone, being widowed, or separating from your partner will usually mean a drop in income. Lone parents tend to be financially worse off than other parents. Many are on welfare benefits and struggle to make ends meet. They are caught in a situation where to get a job would mean paying for childcare, and the money they earned would not be enough to cover this extra cost.

Women are likely to be on a lower income than men. However, Hilary Graham, a researcher who has written about women and poverty, found that for women, being a lone parent could represent not only a different kind of poverty for them, but one that was preferable. This was because the money that was coming in could be controlled directly by the mothers, instead of their being dependent on men for financial decisions. Women's access to, and power over, the household income was seen as the crucial factor in leaving them 'better off poorer'.

Carla has one child aged 12 months:

'Although I was on Income Support, in no way did I feel poor. I had about £200 in savings which made me feel relatively secure and I found I could manage on what I had coming in every week. I had a lot of second-hand clothes given to me and I loved washing, ironing and mending them, in preparation for when my daughter would wear them. It didn't matter that they were second-hand.'

Lone parents can find ways of helping themselves and each other to survive on less money than they are used to.

■ Learning to budget

Learning to budget differently is a skill. This may mean changing spending priorities, for example, putting housing and heating bills first, then paying off loans, then money for buying food. Some local councils or voluntary groups run money advice sessions which anyone can attend. There are many books about managing money — try your local library.

■ Sharing costs with others

Bulk-buying food and household goods with others can save money. Sharing transport, childcare, and practical skills can save time and energy as well. Lone parent groups can be a good source of ideas for cost-cutting and may organise schemes to help members save money.

■ Money is not everything

If you are managing on less money than you are used to, your children may feel hard done by, and put pressure on you to spend more on them. Rather than letting them make you feel guilty, help them to see ways in which they are better off now and emphasise the good things they have.

Managing with disability

Several lone parents who took part in our survey were disabled, or had children with disabilities. This demanded extra skills — both emotional and practical. Knowing that they could not do everything by themselves, they looked to others for support.

Janet has a spinal cord injury, and is paralysed from the waist down:

'There was a five month break in my relationship with my daughter while I was in hospital, but once I returned home things very quickly got back to normal. I did not need any help with looking after her, but I do need help with the housework and this has been a very liberating thing about being disabled. I no longer have to do any housework and can get someone else to do it without feeling guilty.

'It was hard taking up my full-time teaching job when Rena was almost two years old. Although it was very difficult working full-time — not just juggling childcare, but also still getting used to being a wheelchair user — I found that I have a passion for teaching. I also discovered an ability to write when I became involved in a project on the lives of other women with spinal cord injury.'

Janet had to learn to build up her relationship with her daughter after a five month break. She had to learn to ask for help from other people. She had to assess the skills she had and those she needed to learn to manage her disability — for example, being a wheelchair user and developing the muscles in other parts of her body. Through her disability, she discovered new skills — particularly in creative writing.

Marion's middle child is disabled:

'My day starts about 6 am, when I come downstairs to put the kettle on and have "my time". I have a shower and get dressed, while the bath is filling for Peter. Peter is 13 and doubly incontinent: this is the first of possibly three washes a day ... At the end of each day, I check Peter and change his nappy before going to bed myself, usually about midnight. I have to get up at least once in the night to change Peter and quite often his bed linen as well. This is every night of the week and not just once in a while.'

Marion has had to develop skills in order to create time for herself, to be able to wake up and care for her son every night of the week, and to remain optimistic about her life despite her responsibilities.

Sharing responsibility for children and for decisions

In a society where couples are dominant, it is sometimes difficult for lone parents to feel they can bother other people to share in decisions or to help shoulder some of the responsibility of bringing up children. The lone parents who participated in our survey had found different ways of overcoming the heavy load of responsibility. Some had asked for help; others found they got it when they made their situation known to people. Many found their problems shared when they joined a Gingerbread group or another group for lone parents.

Lone parents are in the fortunate position of being free from the 'men's' and 'women's' roles many couples find themselves in. You can learn from others, share your skills and give and take freely. And you can do some of the things you really want to, whether it is fixing cars or baking cakes.

'My neighbours, a lesbian couple with children of their own, were wonderful. One had fought for custody of her child and was really aware of the day-in, day-out responsibility. I was able to call on them at any time and to babysit for their children in return.'

Combining work and childcare

Many people combine work and childcare as a matter of course. But some people find that going out to work cannot be combined with looking after their children, either because the practical difficulties are too great or because paying for childcare reduces their income too much. Some lone parents find that working at home, or returning to study so that they can look forward to better job prospects later, helps them through the years when their children are young.

The women who took part in our survey were more inclined than the men to feel guilty about working outside the home. Women are often afraid that their children will suffer if they do not stay at home to look after them when they are young. There is absolutely no evidence for this.

Men, on the other hand, were more likely to feel guilty if they could not take on paid work. They expect to earn money as well as being parents, so they feel less guilty about finding and paying for childcare.

Beating isolation and loneliness

Lone parents often mentioned loneliness as a problem. Many had been able to break out of their isolation by joining a lone parent group, by finding reliable babysitters so that they could get out to see friends, by asking friends over to visit, by using the telephone to keep in touch with friends, or by taking home study courses.

'The time when I get really lonely is usually late at night and when I least expect it. So I go to bed because things always seem better in the morning. If it happens during the day I go out to my sister's or my next-door neighbour's, or I clean the cupboards, bake a cake, read or watch a video.'

'I get out my diary and try to fill up the weeks with things to look forward to.'

'I ring a friend, write a letter or get the kids to give me a cuddle.'

'There isn't anything that fills that deeper loneliness for someone very close. I just acknowledge the pain, have a cry if necessary, and then get on with life.'

If you are able to accept that you will have periods of loneliness, you can plan what to do when these times occur. It is also worth remembering that some of the loneliness comes from the need for adult contact, and your children cannot satisfy this.

New roles: new skills

Being a lone parent opens up opportunities to learn new skills and take on new roles free from traditional stereotypes. It can also set new examples to children about how women and men behave.

Think about the things that you do well now, but you would never have thought you could do before you became a lone parent. They can be things to do with your children, your household, your workplace, yourself. You can list them here.

Marcia's list
- I can now decorate quite well and even lay carpets.
- I provide a comfortable home.
- I have helped my children to develop their interests in ways that bring out their best characteristics.
- I now control my own life, with three children to be responsible for as well.

Sam's list
- I can now cook decent meals.
- I can buy my children's clothes.
- I have learned to manage all the household chores.
- I can take responsibility for my children.

Anne's list
- I approach other people for help.
- I can give the housework a miss without feeling guilty, even when visitors come.
- I go to school functions on my own.
- I'm more assertive than I used to be.
- I can mix easily with a group of strangers.

Diana's list
- I am in control of my own life.
- I keep a clean and healthy home.
- I am no longer worried about approaching large organisations, friends, etc, for assistance.
- I can stand up for my rights.

Men who answered our questionnaire said that they experienced a variety of changes when they became lone parents. Some said that they had given up work to be with their children. Some had discovered things about themselves they had not known, or had learned parenting skills they had not needed before. Others had taken on paid housekeeping and childcare help — thus replacing the female partner who had filled this role — but had still had to learn to be 'more of a parent' than they were before.

'I had to learn to use the washing machine. In 10 years I had never touched it.'

'How do you shop for clothes? Especially for daughters' clothes?'

'Planning how much shopping to buy for four people was difficult. I either bought too much or we ran out at the worst time.'

'I was too mixed up with my own feelings to notice that my youngest child was really suffering. I was not used to noticing her moods. Now I am.'

While men reported difficulties with things like taking young daughters to public toilets, knowing what to do when daughters began their periods, and so on, they also found rewards in being able to manage a household and cope with children and domestic chores — tasks normally considered women's work. Their children, too, learned that men could do all these things and be caring and nurturing, thus giving them a new view of a man's role.

Women in our survey who had become lone parents after a relationship ended, overwhelmingly said that they felt liberated by aspects of being a lone parent, even if they had been widowed. Often they had been in relationships where their needs had had to take second place to those of their partners, and their identity was lost under that of wife and mother. Many had been denied a career or job prospects, leisure interests and educational opportunities. Lone parenthood allowed them the chance to rebuild these. We asked them what they felt their children had learned about male and female roles since being alone.

'I think children accept a dual role by the one parent. It also makes children form different ideas as they grow up. They realise that a woman's place is not always in the kitchen, nor a man's out at work.'

'My kids see me doing DIY, driving the car, mending the loo, and other traditionally male tasks.'

'I hope Sally is learning from our situation that she is capable of doing anything and that women are not the "weaker" sex. She helps me with all sorts of things that would normally be done by a man. She also sees that things are not easy.'

'I think that my daughter will grow up with a positive view of women, since there is no task I will not try. She sees me do the housework, handle the money, decorate the house, do the garden, make shelves, mend cars, play rough games, cuddle, laugh, shout, get angry, and so on. I hope she assumes that men do all this too. She has seen my dad do most of these things.'

Even if traditional sex-role defined tasks no longer apply to you, there will be some things that you cannot or will not tackle — at least, not at the moment.

'I still can't summon the nerve to walk into a pub by myself.'

'Having to use sexual charm to get things done really annoys me. My jaws hurt from grinning.'

'As a man I find that things that happen during the daytime are mainly for women, and I feel out of place being the only man.'

It could be that you still lack practical skills:

'I'll never get used to ironing.'

'Manual jobs around the house are beyond me.'

You may still have to learn to deal with situations you have never had to think about before:

'It's hard to find support in dealing with my children's problems.'

'I don't know how to deal with my daughter asking about her father.'

Getting the skills you want

One way of starting to make changes is to look at the skills you have and the skills you need. Use the chart below to help you.

Write down the skills you need in the first column. In the second column, put your own suggestions, and those of other people, for how to go about getting these skills. Use the third column to check your progress and note what you have achieved.

Some of the things you want to do may seem out of reach. One lone parent who wrote to us gave this advice, which others found helpful:

'If there are matters I can't solve, I split the problem into five or six small solvable problems and go through them one by one.'

Lone parenting can be liberating — the people we surveyed were sure of that — but you need to take advantage of the changes it can bring. The experience of others suggests you should throw out the old patterns that are not useful to you as a lone parent, recognise the skills you have or could learn, and share responsibility around a bit.

Contacts

Citizens Advice Bureau for advice on benefits, etc. Look in the phone book under 'Citizens Advice' or try phoning the National Association of Citizens Advice Bureaux on London (071) 833 2181.

Department of Social Security for leaflets on benefits. Look in the phone book under 'Social Security' or 'Health and Social Security'.

Freeline Social Security is a free DSS telephone enquiry service — call 0800 666555 (freephone).

Gingerbread has leaflets on benefits. Their advice worker is available from 2 to 5 pm, Monday to Friday, for advice on all aspects of lone parenting. Ring London (071) 240 0953.

What I need	Suggestions for how to get it	What you did, when, response received; what still needs to be done

3 Getting help and support

'Getting support is sometimes easier said than done. Swallow your pride, but don't wait until you have a crisis. It's easier to start off with something small like a chat.'

Everyone needs help and support from other people, and as a lone parent you are no different. The amount of help and support you ask for and are offered may depend on how you came to be a lone parent, how long you have been on your own, the help and support you already have, and whether you are a woman or a man. This chapter will help you think about:

- when you need help and support
- who you can call on
- how people can help and support each other
- what help and support you can give to others.

By 'help and support' we mean both practical help with things like mending a cooker, babysitting, shopping, looking after children or finding somewhere to live — and emotional support, such as sympathetic listening, good advice, a shoulder to cry on, or having fun together.

Who can you turn to?

Look through the list of situations on the right, and decide who you would go to for support if you needed it.

People you could go to might include:

- family/relatives
- friends
- lovers
- your children's teachers
- other parents
- leisure contacts
- people at your church/temple/synagogue
- neighbours
- housing workers
- counselling service
- shopkeepers
- social services workers
- childcare workers
- health visitors, doctors
- community workers
- lone parent group members
- ex-partner.

When might you need support?

- ❏ Your children are behaving badly a lot of the time.
- ❏ You are too ill to get out of bed one morning.
- ❏ You are asked out and need a babysitter at short notice.
- ❏ You are offered a really good job, and need to find someone to care for the children.
- ❏ Your children are ill and you have to go to work.
- ❏ The car will not start in the morning.
- ❏ Your child is being racially abused by local children.
- ❏ You are taken ill at work.
- ❏ It is one o'clock in the morning and you feel terribly depressed.
- ❏ You get the chance to go away for a weekend without the children.
- ❏ You do not have enough money to buy the evening meal.
- ❏ Your children need help with their school work, which you are not able to give them.
- ❏ You generally feel low in spirits.
- ❏ The cooker breaks down.
- ❏ Your home needs repairs or decorating.
- ❏ You are frightened of burglars in the night.
- ❏ Your wheelchair-pusher goes on holiday for two weeks.

No-one to turn to?

If you do not feel there are people you can call on, there are three things you can try:

● Ring Gingerbread's London office for the name and phone number of the contact person for your nearest group, or for help from Gingerbread's advice worker.
● Look on the notice-board at the local library, health centre or community centre for groups you could join or helplines you could phone.
● Ask the local citizens advice bureau for advice or helping services you could use.

Do you depend too much on one or two people?

Think about whether you could widen your list of 'supporters'. One lone parent put up a notice at her children's school inviting other people for coffee on a Thursday morning. She made three new friends this way, two of them also lone parents. Another parent volunteered to supervise swimming at the local sports centre and now teaches classes quite regularly — and gets paid. He was also able to join a sports instructors' group where he made a couple of good friends.

You probably found that you looked to lots of different people and services for support. We asked Gingerbread members and others where their support had come from when they first became lone parents. Chart 1 shows their replies.

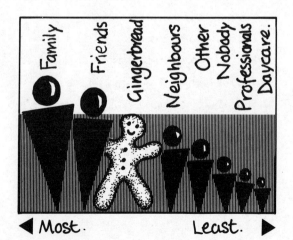

Another group of lone parents talked about the people who gave them most support now. They had a similar list shown in chart 2.

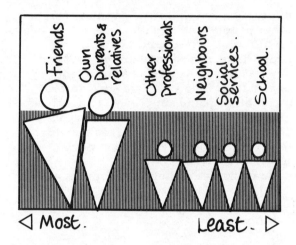

In both cases, friends and relatives came over as the most important sources of support. You have a right to ask for support from your family. Friends will want to help you because they gain something from your friendship. Groups for lone parents can often help you make new friends. Some people feel as though a group like this replaces or adds to their family. Children can also provide a great deal of support.

What all of this shows is how important it is for you to keep in touch with relatives, and to value and make an effort at friendships. It is sometimes easy to let friendships lapse, and to keep out of the way of your family. When you are depressed you may find it hard to believe that anyone would want to be your friend. Or perhaps you feel that your family would have no sympathy, or that you would not be able to meet their expectations. But unless you ask, people do not know you need them; so give them a chance.

Your supporters

Below is a list of some of the ways in which lone parents have found that people give support. Look through the list, and write in the names of the people who provide this kind of support for you. We have given some examples, but you can add your own. People may appear a number of times on your list.

Ways people give support

Type of support

- A roof over my head
- Lending/giving me things
- Help with budgeting
- Buying things for the children

- Sorting out benefits
- Running errands
- Taking me shopping
- Decorating/home maintenance

- Doing housework for me
- Taking us/me out
- Helping when I'm ill
- Looking after the children

- Providing services at a cheaper rate
- Providing free or cheap activities
- Coming with me to see my solicitor
- Helping me see I can do things on my own

- Praising and encouraging me
- Being there when I need them
- Listening/understanding
- Telephoning me

- Coming to live with me
- Letting me shout at her
- Visiting me/ providing companionship
- Asking me to join club/activities/go out

- Providing a social life
- Asking me over for meals

Who gives it

Now take your list of people who have helped you and make a 'map' of your supporters, like the four lone parents' 'maps' shown here and on the next page.

Put yourself in the centre, then, close to your name, put the names of the people who support you most. Further away, put the names of people who support you less.

Making a map like this does not mean you make judgments about who is better at providing help and support for you. It just helps you work out who is around and how much use you make of them. It may help you see if you need or want to make changes. Add everyone you can think of who is important to you. You may be surprised how many people you know.

Looking at the gaps

The four lone parents whose maps we have shown used this exercise to work out ways to fill the gaps they found in their support.

These included:

● not being afraid to tell people about the good things that happen rather than just the bad: people might be pleased to share in your happiness
● deciding to make more demands on the friends they already had
● widening their circle of friends and acquaintances by looking up old friends and joining groups and clubs where they could meet new ones.

Fiona

'I realised that I have plenty of practical support when things go wrong, but nobody who I feel I can just ring and say, "Hey, something good has happened to me". I must allow people to get closer to me and let myself ask for more support, as people assume I am good at coping and do not see that at times I am desperate for help.'

Makbul

'It showed me how many people I did know, as well as showing me that I only really have a limited circle of good friends. I was surprised at how much I did for other people. I think I'll ask them to help me a bit more.'

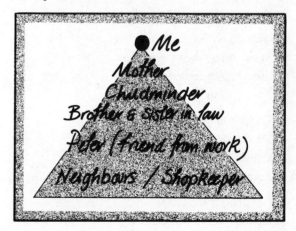

Denise

'I can see that I have many acquaintances but few true friends. I don't really want to change things. My friend Anne is always there when I need her but for some things I rely on the group I belong to. There are times you need someone to talk to but only certain people can help.'

Shabnam

'It looks as though I've cut myself off from couples, old friends, etc, because all my present friends are lone parents from Gingerbread. I'm going to get my address book out and look people up. I'm also going to widen my interests and go to night school to meet other categories of people.'

Not all lone parents will need to look for new sources of support. Making a map like this may help you realise that you do not want to change the support you have.

Find it hard to ask for support?

'No-one will look down on you. Ask for support. It's very often gladly given and it will ease the pressures on you and the children.'

'It's easy to slip into making an outward show that things are alright because you are wary of saying "I can't cope". Since I've looked for more support from the people I know, my life has opened up. And I still give help to other people in my turn — some of whom I have been helping for a long time.'

You may have become so used to caring for other people that it is hard to care for yourself. You may not think you deserve care and attention.

On the other hand, you may have relied on a partner to do all the caring in your family, so that providing emotional support for others is a skill you may have to develop. You may also have been brought up to think it is 'weak' to ask for help — but it is weaker not to try and change things for the better.

Asking for support does not mean that you are weak or cannot cope. It does not mean that you will become dependent on other people. It means that at this particular moment you have a need, and a right, to ask other people for help. You can 'pay back' that help as soon as you are able, in a way that suits you.

Giving as well as getting

Support works both ways. When you give support you get something in return. But this 'something' is different for different people. For some it might mean swopping services — you look after a friend's child for an afternoon one week, they do the same for you the week after. Others get their reward from the pleasure of knowing they have made someone happy or made themselves useful. So nothing is expected in return because the pleasure is in the 'doing'. Family and relatives can be expected to offer support, and can expect the same of you too. Friends may support you because they get pleasure from your company and are pleased to do things for you. Again, there may be no expectation of being paid back.

Everyone on your support map probably also counts on your support in some way. To check on the support you offer others, look again at the list of *Ways people give support*, on page 27. Put a tick by the kinds of support you feel you offer other people. Are there any surprises?

Louise

'I was surprised at how much support I do give to other people. I looked back over the last couple of months and found:

- *I'd had three friends to stay with me*
- *I'd looked after other people's children on 12 occasions*
- *I'd listened to lots of people's moans in shops, outside the school, in the pub*
- *I'd let other people use my phone on several occasions.*

'The list of people I'd supported was very long, so why didn't I feel I could ask anyone for support when I needed it? I decided to phone up the two nearest friends and ask them for a bit of their time. They both seemed pleased! Later one of them said, "You always seem to cope so well we didn't realise you could do with help too!".'

Carlos

'I suppose I hadn't counted the time I spent with other men as support. We always seem to be doing things or talking about things that don't matter, rather than anything deeper. We never talked about feelings and relationships — I didn't even know whether some of them had children! I'd relied on women to give me support with the children and with my feelings. One evening I got talking to one of the other group members, and found out he had brought up two children alone for three years so he knew what I was coping with. He says he's often at a loose end at the weekends and would like some company. I feel better just for sharing it all.'

Contacts

Parentline — OPUS is a helpline run by parents for parents experiencing difficulties. Call London (081) 645 0469.

Samaritans provide counselling for people in distress. Look under Samaritans in the phone book, or ask Directory Enquiries.

Relate (formerly National Marriage Guidance Council) offers counselling to anyone, not just to married couples. Ask Directory Enquiries or ring their national office on 0788 73241.

Family Helpline, run by the National Children's Home. Ask Directory Enquiries for your local number.

Cruse — Bereavement Care offers counselling for bereaved people. Call London (081) 940 4818.

British Association for Counselling for information about local counselling services. Ring 0788 78328/9.

4 Your children's feelings

'My sons and I are very close now. They know I love them very much, and they have got over the fear that I will leave them, too.'

'When my relationship ended, my 5 year old daughter was very upset. But I'm afraid I was going through such turmoil at the time that I didn't notice her anxiety. It is only now when I look back at photos and see how unhappy she looked that I realise what she went through.'

When adult relationships end, parents are often, quite naturally, full of their own needs. Sometimes the children can be forgotten. But becoming a lone parent family affects your children as well as you. This chapter looks at children's feelings after a separation or the death of a parent.

Adults may be unaware of how easily children, of whatever age, can sense the changes which occur when parents separate. Many people think that their children are 'too young' to know what is happening. But they do respond to changes by behaving differently.

'When my child was 8 months old I left her father, because he had been violent towards me. We moved in with friends of mine. Even though she was very small, I believe she sensed the change in environment and the tension I felt. She became very unsettled and cried every time it came to putting her coat on; it was as if she didn't know where she was going to, and whether I'd be collecting her.'

Jacqueline Burgoyne carried out a number of research studies on divorce. In her book *Divorce matters* she reported that very few children want their parents to split up, and that it is rare for a child to welcome a separation. She also made the point that children do not choose to have their parents separate: the decision is imposed on them. She did not say this to make parents feel guilty for separating. She wanted to make them realise that while they believe they are doing what is best for them and therefore for all the family, the children may not feel this at all.

'Many, if not most, parents seem to believe that the less said to children the better, a point that is contradicted by research studies. If little is said to children, they often get a very distorted idea of what is happening and have little or no opportunity to talk about their fears and fantasies. For others there is an opportunity for discussion and to ask questions.'

Jacqueline Burgoyne also emphasised that children react differently to separation depending on:

- their age
- the kind of children they are
- how they deal with difficulties
- their relationships with their parents
- their own expectations of family life.

The circumstances that surround the separation are also important:

'My husband had been gone for a year before we told Michael that he no longer lived with us. Mike was only 3 when Dan left and was already used to him being away, as he had to travel so much for work. More often than not he was only home at weekends. So because Mike still saw Dan every weekend, life for him was kept as normal as possible and I don't think he really noticed much change. I remember that I really worked hard to keep up routines.'

It is not being part of a one parent family that causes children's distress, but the feelings they experience that come from having to put up with something they did not want to happen. It is important to separate the two, so as not to fall into the trap of believing that children are 'deprived' because they are from lone parent families. Almost all of the separated lone parents who took part in our survey said that they and their children were doing well, showing that it is possible to get over anger and bad feelings.

Getting closer to your children

Talking to your children is an obvious way of getting close to them. Listening carefully to their comments and questions can also help you find out what they are thinking, and whether they understand the situation. With some young children, you can find out what is on their minds by playing games with them, or drawing pictures together. Or you could get them to talk to a pet or favourite toy about what is happening in the family.

Noticing children's behaviour

Noticing and watching your children's behaviour can also give you clues as to how they are feeling. Try the following exercise to get you thinking.

Look at the following list of ways children might behave. For each one, try to decide what feelings might lie behind the behaviour.

Your children:
- do not want to bring their friends home
- say they have not told people that their parents have split up
- are more clinging than usual with you
- cry much more than usual
- do not want to be left alone
- are not sleeping well at night
- are wetting the bed regularly
- are fussy about their food
- are not eating properly
- are talking 'baby talk'
- are asking questions like:
  — 'Will we see gran and grandpa again?'
  — 'Will we have to move and leave the dog behind?'

Now think about how your children reacted when you and your partner separated and the feelings that were behind their behaviour. Make a note of this below.

Understanding how children feel at any time can help you be more aware of their fears and anxieties.

What are these feelings?

■ Feeling guilty and responsible

A number of people writing about children and their parents' separation have noted that some children blame themselves for the split and need constantly to be told that they are not to blame. They give examples of children who feel they have caused their parent's death or departure by being naughty or having an argument with the person just before she or he died or left. Adults also have these feelings, but children's age and lack of experience make it important that they should not be left feeling responsible.

However, opinions do differ about what lies behind children's distress. Jacqueline Burgoyne did not find that children blamed themselves for their parents' separation. She thought that the children became upset because they resented the decision their parents had made, and felt they were powerless to stop it.

Whoever the children feel is to blame, it is clear that they need to make sense of what is happening and that parents should help them to do this.

■ Feeling angry

Children may take their anger out on their parents if they resent the decision to separate. How they do this will depend on their age and how much they are used to talking about their feelings.

'He is prone to occasional temper tantrums towards me.'

'She grew quite hostile towards me at times and then she would say it was all my fault that her dad had gone to live with another woman.'

'Kevin showed no reaction for about six months, but then became very aggressive to me, very hateful and hurtful. He ran away twice, which involved the police, and it took a good year of reassurance to make him realise that I am not going away and that we both still love him.'

It seems that in many cases, while the children really want to direct the anger and hurt at the parent who has left, they take it out on the parent they live with.

Children's anger may be complicated by the fear that if they are angry with one or both parents, it may drive the parents away. In this situation, the anger could become a dangerous feeling which is hidden, instead of being expressed. It can also lead a child to feel guilty for having bad feelings about someone they love.

- Do not meet children's anger with your own. It only makes the situation worse instead of getting to the cause of the anger.

- Tell the children that you can see that they are upset and you want to talk about why. Encourage them to talk about their feelings. For example, they may be disappointed or angry with the absent parent for not coming to their school party because other children had two parents there. It may take time and patience to get them to tell you this, but it is worth it if it helps them not to bottle up their feelings.

- Explain to the children that getting angry or upset is not going to change the basic situation. Show them ways of dealing with their feelings, such as punching a pillow, kicking a ball, yelling into a cupboard, or jumping up and down.

- Try doing the opposite to what you feel towards them. For example, give them a kiss when you feel like smacking them. This works, but only if it is unexpected.

■ Feeling that they might be left or abandoned

If one parent has left or died, children often fear that they will lose the other one too.

'My husband had died suddenly in the night. Our daughter Elaine was afraid whenever I was away from her that I might have died too. It seemed to make things easier when we counted up all the people who loved Elaine and would care for her if I wasn't there. I also arranged for our neighbour, Reena, to teach Elaine her phone number. This reassured Elaine that Reena was there if she was needed, and that they had a plan that would work, if anything did ever happen to me.'

Other behaviour associated with these feelings includes children clinging, not settling at bedtime, not wanting to go to school, or panicking if they cannot find you when, for example, you are out shopping together. Children who feel like this need to be reassured often by your words and your actions, that they are not going to be left. For example, avoid being late back when you go out, or disappearing without letting them know where you have gone. This insecurity should lessen as time goes on.

■ Feeling bereaved

People do not always realise that children may grieve when parents separate just as much as they would if a parent had died. Children react to loss and show grief in different ways.

'For weeks after my husband left, we couldn't seem to get warm, the shock made us shiver and huddle together in a vain attempt to get warm. As the weeks go by, the nightmares and the night-time screams for daddy have gradually faded away, the laughter and the sparkle in their eyes is returning. Billy has stopped day-dreaming at school. Life is becoming relaxed and the sun is beginning to shine again.'

'Darren who is 16 tried to show no emotion at all. "Big boys don't cry" seemed to be his attitude. I explained to him that nobody would think any less of him if he didn't bottle up his feelings. It was obvious he was suffering as much as I was.

'Tracey who is 14 cried herself to sleep every night for two weeks holding a photograph of her mother ... Denise who is 6 shed a few tears in the first couple of days. Since then she regularly asks questions about how and why it happened. I answer her as honestly as I can.'

'It's taken me four years to accept what happened in my life and early on I was often "downright negative" about it all, so I didn't explain well to my children and often lost my temper if they mentioned "it".'

■ Feeling change and loss in other ways

As well as losing a parent, some children lose other familiar things in their lives. Many have to leave their homes and possessions, their friends and neighbours and their schools. This can affect them a great deal.

'During the first eighteen months we moved four times, but their school remained the same. I had a lot of problems with them when we moved to a town about thirty miles away. Mainly, I think, this was because they lost their school friends and felt unsettled. They reacted very differently. The elder boy was very rude in school to adults and quite unruly. The younger one became quiet and withdrawn.'

Giving your children information about what is happening, and why, is important. Helping them to see the good points of any change can allow your children (and you) to plan ahead. If it is possible to keep in touch with friends, relatives and schools by post or telephone this can ease the loss. If you have the energy to involve your children in social activities, clubs and groups, this can also help them to adjust.

'My children reacted very well. I had been to see the Welfare Department at the Council and they offered to put us in the hostel. By this time the children were picking up vibes from me and did get upset, but then I had the bright idea of telling them that we were going on holiday and started singing etc. I had no idea at all what situation we

were going to. When we arrived at the hostel and I had found out a bit more, I told the children that we were going to stay in a "holiday flat" and they were fine — settled in beautifully. To this day they still call the hostel "holiday flat". The twins were then 3 and the baby was 16 months.'

Questions children ask

■ Children who have never known their other parent

These are the kinds of questions children may ask:

'Where is he?'
'Why doesn't she live here with us?'
'Doesn't he love me?'
'Other children have daddies, why don't I?'

And this is how some lone parents have dealt with the questions:

'I've always been a lone parent. My daughter has never seen her father and when I hear about custody disagreements and parental arguments and confused kids, I think I'm in a better position, since this is one hassle I don't have. Louise has commented, though, that other children have daddies and that she hasn't. I told her that she did have a daddy but we don't see him. When she asked why, I told her that after he'd helped me to make her, he decided he didn't want to be a daddy after all. This has come up several times and I've tried to point to all the different family backgrounds we know and to emphasise who she does love — grandad, grandma, uncle and mummy. I've encouraged her to be close to the men in my family because I want her to grow up with a positive image of men and I think my dad and brother will provide this.'

'The subject has always been openly discussed and my daughter seems to have taken it in her stride. I have gone to lengths to ensure she does not conjure up a romantic hero for her absent father. She tends to think other children are the unlucky ones because she lives with her grandparents and they don't. At 5 years old, the other children agree she's lucky. If you appear to take it in your stride, the children happily discuss it all, and it doesn't become a big deal.'

■ Children whose parent has died

Children are likely to ask questions such as these:

'Where has mummy gone?'
'Why won't daddy come back?'
'Will you go away too?'

How you answer questions about death will depend very much on your religious and spiritual beliefs, as well as how comfortable you feel talking about it. On the whole, children are not encouraged to discuss death or to see people who have died, even in peaceful circumstances. It is important that children's questions about death do get answered, though, rather than brushed aside.

This is how some lone parents have answered:

'I told them that God had taken daddy away to live with him because he could look after his illness better than we could. I told them although we were sad, daddy was happier because he was well, but that I was sure he missed us.'

'How do you explain suicide to a child? I told her that mummy was so unhappy with herself that she didn't want to make us unhappy too. So she decided to leave us forever so we wouldn't worry about her anymore. People told me later that this was not a good way to explain suicide to a child, but it was all I could think of.'

■ Children who still have contact with the other parent

Questions children may ask in this situation are:

'Why can't you, mummy and me live together?'
'Why doesn't daddy love me?'
'If daddy gets married again, will he still be my daddy?'
'Why won't mummy come to see my school play?'
'When will my dad finish his job and come to see me?'

And here are some ways parents have replied:

'I have explained that it is horrid to live with adults who argue a lot as my parents did and still do. I also stress the advantages of two families and having the weekly visit to her father's house where she is loved and experiences a different sort of domestic situation. I always stress that we all love her dearly.'

'I try to explain it wouldn't work and we would all be terribly hurt. They reply that they can't be more hurt than they are now. My eldest son feels this very acutely. He is very frustrated by seeing two people he loves and sees as "nice people" not being able to love each other. He cannot understand this and wants to put it right.'

'My children have asked if I like their mum and why we don't live together. I replied that mum and I don't get on any more and couldn't live together because we kept arguing.'

'At first he really didn't talk about it, then he couldn't understand why his father didn't love him, which of course he did. I explained quite honestly that his father had found someone else, and my son accepted this until his father remarried when, for a time, he thought that meant he didn't have a daddy any more.'

'They do, however, wish he would come to school plays, outings, etc (but I believe that even with married couples, husbands often do not attend events of this kind). To help children feel positive about the home situation, I tell them that we're a "special" family, with added strengths and rewards. I stress that they are very much loved by both parents and grandparents and that the breakup of the relationship was no fault of theirs.'

'He lives a long way away. But when you're older, perhaps you'll be able to go and see him.'

Being positive

These are some general principles that came out of the suggestions we received.

- Provide honest and accurate information to children in ways they can understand. They particularly like to know practical things — like where they will sleep, who will look after them, whether they can see friends or relatives, whether they can have toys and other familiar things around.

- Talk openly with children so that they can make sense of what is going on.

- Give children the chance to air their feelings and their worries about the present, and the future. Give them the chance to talk about what others might say to them and how they could answer people's questions.

- Keep the children as secure as possible, and their lives as unchanged as possible in other ways.

- Help children keep their own identities by encouraging contact with their friends, relatives and others who care for them. Black children growing up with a white parent need to have their blackness valued and reinforced. White parents can do this by keeping contact with their black in-laws and other black people.

- Tell the children frequently that you love them.

We asked lone parents what their advice would be. Here are some of the suggestions:

'I don't think you can make the children feel positive about being in a one parent family unless you feel positive yourself. You can bring the children up as you think best, without arguments, and the children can have two homes and the best of both worlds.'

'I would say be honest with your child. It's bloody hard being a lone parent — you don't have to be a martyr, just listen to your kid, be honest about what you say and feel and need, and then get on with loving her/him.'

'Be truthful about everything and don't be bitter when talking to the children. Let them know what's happening and that it is upsetting. Separation can be painful. But you can overcome this if you want. If you get on with life and don't let the past get you down you can end up happy and contented. It all takes time and that is something we have.'

'I think people should reassure their children that they are still a family and do things that all families do. Gingerbread groups are wonderful because they don't allow you to forget this.'

Dealing with worrying situations

Below are a number of situations you may find yourself in with your children. In each case, think about why the child is behaving like this. What would you do or say?

- Your 5 year old who has just started school comes home in tears with scratches on her face. She has been fighting, and says, *'They say we are not a family because I haven't got a daddy/mummy.'*

- Your 8 year old is constantly complaining that he cannot have the toys and books he wants and that 'all' his friends at school have them.

- Your 4 year old and 7 year old get very upset before they visit their other parent. When they return, they are always very quiet.

- Your 7 year old comes home and says, *'They say you're not my mother because I'm black and you're not.'*

- Your 12 year old used to have many friends and lots of interests. He now stays at home a great deal and watches television. He says, *'I don't feel like doing anything any more now that mummy isn't here.'*

- Your 16 year old says, *'If you don't let me buy the clothes I want, I'm going to tell dad when I see him this weekend that you're not using his money for us.'*

What can you do?

- If the children feel hurt or anxious, or have experienced prejudice from outside the family, they need to be listened to and reassured they are not to blame. Ridiculing, teasing, criticising or threatening them will not make things better. Instead, any wrong information should be corrected and explained. The child should know who she or he can go to for support.

- Any behaviour which is clearly wrong — violence or being rude and angry; playing one parent off against the other — should be recognised for what it is, and the children told clearly that it is not the way to get what they want.

- Tell the children how *you* feel. Many adults find it difficult to talk about their feelings to their children. They may be afraid that they would lose control and the children would see them in distress. Sometimes there is a fear of 'losing face' with the children — adults are supposed to be strong and able to cope. Sometimes they want to protect their children from the extreme emotions involved in their distress as these may be painful for the children too.

- Many of the lone parents who wrote to us found that they became closer to their children when they shared their sorrow (but see *Leaning on your children* on this page).

- Everyone who writes about the break up of relationships seems to agree that parents should not let their bitterness or anger about their ex-partner affect their child's relationship with the absent parent. This means not undermining each other; not running the other parent down; not asking the child to take sides and blame the other partner. If these things happen, the children suffer.

Leaning on your children

A number of lone parents who wrote to us realised that they were depending on their children more than they should:

'I feel I ask their opinion on things perhaps a bit too much so that we are almost making a joint decision over things.'

One lone parent remembered how it was when she was a child and her parents separated:

'I always looked to my parents for stability and comfort. Suddenly the tables were turned. I was the one being looked to for comfort and stability.'

There is a difference between involving your children in discussions and confiding in them; between sharing some responsibility with them, and relying on them to take the main responsibility for decisions. No matter how mature they seem, they do not have the experience to be your emotional equals. They need to spend time with other children, and you need other adults to rely on.

Contacts

Exploring Parenthood runs workshops for parents. Ring London (071) 607 9647.

Parentline — OPUS is a helpline run by parents. Call London (081) 645 0469.

Parent Network is a national network helping to improve relationships between parents and children. Ring London (071) 485 8535.

5 Your children's other parent

'I think we have a better relationship since the divorce. The girls seem to like having two homes, and two parents who actually enjoy being with them. I trust his judgment, knowing he's not going to undermine my decisions about bringing up the children. And I know I could count on him in any crisis.'

'When my marriage broke up my younger child couldn't understand why her father wanted to live somewhere else, not with us. She asked, "Why can't he be our daddy any more?" I try to reassure her — "Of course he's still your daddy" — but it starts to wear thin as his visits become less frequent and his behaviour falls short of the children's expectations.'

'I always made a point of talking to Isaac about the fun I had while he was away with his father. I did this because I wanted him to understand that I had a life of my own, and also I didn't want him to feel guilty or disloyal about enjoying himself without me.'

There is much evidence to show that children gain from keeping in contact with both parents, where this is possible, and that it is generally to everyone's advantage to set up arrangements for the children to do this. This chapter focuses on ways of helping to make these arrangements run smoothly.

An arrangement may be voluntary, or it may have been laid down by the court. Either way, it is usually called 'access' although the 1989 Children Act has altered the law relating to children, including the law on custody and access. The law used to mention 'custody' and 'care and control', so that children were seen to live with one of the parents, and the other one just had 'access'. The new law talks of 'parental responsibility' and 'contact orders', which determine how much time each parent spends with the children, and parents will, in future, be expected to negotiate more. But the old term, 'access', will probably be used for a long time to come, and we are using it in this chapter.

Access arrangements are set up in order to continue relationships between children and both of their parents. The purpose is not to maintain relationships between ex-partners. Sometimes the adults need to remember this.

Children benefit from regular and reliable arrangements to help them feel secure and cared for. Adults benefit from the time they have to themselves while the children are away. So even though good arrangements can be difficult to set up and keep going, they are worth it for everyone.

This chapter is based on four case studies of families who have made access arrangements. In each case we have tried to examine the arrangements from the different points of view of the people involved.

As you read through the case studies, think about these different viewpoints. There are questions at the end of each case study that you might like to discuss with other adults and perhaps with your children.

Janice and Peter

Janice left her husband Peter, suddenly, when their children, Dan and Lisa, were 9 months old and 3 years old. For six months she lived on her own and they heard nothing from her; then she made contact again.

Peter could not forgive Janice for leaving him. He was totally unprepared for the task of looking after the children, and had to give up his job to do so. When she asked for custody, he fought her in the courts and won: she did not have a permanent address or a job; she was the one who had deserted the family; he had the family home and had given up work to care for the children.

Janice was granted access every weekend and for half the school holidays. Peter does not encourage the children to visit her: he claims that the children are doing well without her and find the visits upsetting. Janice has built up a comfortable life with plenty of friends and a good job. The children love being with her.

Peter

'I will never forgive her for abandoning the children. No normal mother would have done this so, in my view, she's not fit to bring up the children. I said so in the court, but they still granted her access. Why should she get away with it? I'd like to stop her seeing them because, even though they want to go with her, they are always disturbed when they get back. It's not good for them. Now that she's got a place of her own I bet she'll go back to the courts and ask for custody; they favour women anyway.'

Janice

'I feel wretched. Nobody understood how much it took to get up and leave, how the life I was living was stifling me. Peter did not want to know. He was satisfied, and couldn't see what I had to feel dissatisfied about. These last two years have torn me apart. I can't live without the children. He's done a good job with the children, but his hatred and his refusal to understand are so hurtful — and the children sense that. Lisa, who's 6, can't cope with it at all. She tells me what her daddy

says about me and can see with her own eyes that it's not true. But she feels confused and mixed up about her loyalties.'*

Lisa (aged 6)

'I don't like it when daddy's angry and mummy's sad. When we come back from mummy's, daddy gets very cross and shouts a lot. Dan cries all the time then. I want to see mummy and daddy. Daddy won't let us bring anything back from mummy's house.'

- Should access be granted to a parent who 'deserts' children like this?
- Does it make any difference whether the parent who leaves is the mother or father?
- How might it affect the children, if this situation carries on?
- How could Peter and Janice improve or resolve the situation?

When there is hostility between parents, children can be pulled in opposite directions. Sometimes parents are so full of bitterness and resentment they forget their children's needs. Parents should not channel their anger with each other into battles over their children. Children should not be forced into a situation where they feel they have to choose which parent they prefer. They have a right to love each parent separately and differently. If they feel they have to hide the fact that they enjoy being with the other parent, or cannot talk about the good time they had, they will learn mistrust, deception, and feel insecure.

Women who leave their children are often judged more harshly than men. Some of Peter's bitterness seems to stem from a belief that women should not leave their children, and if they do, they deserve to be punished. Peter seems to be using the children's signs of distress when they return from their mother's as ammunition to 'prove' that the children prefer living with him. In reality, they are expressing their discomfort at the parents' relationship. One parent wrote: *'He encourages our daughter to be upset, because it makes him feel more wanted.'*

Sharon and Paul

Sharon had her son when she was 17. She and the child's father, Paul, still live in the same town. Sharon and the baby lived with her parents for a year while she went to college, then got a council house which they share with another lone parent and her child.

Paul never told his parents about the baby and has only seen his son a few times, although the baby is now 16 months old.

Sharon takes up the story

'He knows the baby is his, but it's as if he doesn't want to admit it. It's like he's trying to shut the whole thing out of his life. I would never stop him from seeing his son, as I would like my child to relate to his own father. I feel as if my baby is missing a lot. He only knows one set of grandparents because Paul hasn't told his parents: I think he's too scared to. I did threaten once to tell Paul's mother, but he got very angry.

I got very upset after the baby was born, because Paul refused to be named on the birth certificate. When I phoned him to get him to come with me to register the baby he said that to be put on the birth certificate is to be a real father and he wasn't going to be that to my son. I try not to get angry with him. I'm even polite to him when I see him, because it's just not worth the effort.'

Paul's version

'I'm not ready to be a father yet. Besides, I don't have a proper job and I live with my parents. I think she should have had an abortion but she wouldn't. I would have paid some money to have it done. So it was her decision to have the kid. I get embarrassed when I see her, in case everyone knows. I think some of my friends have guessed but they haven't let on. I've got nothing against the kid, you know, but I'm just too young to settle down. Maybe in a few years' time I'll be ready to get to know him.'

- Should a child have the right to know who her/his parents and grandparents are?
- Should Sharon try to get Paul to have more contact with his child?
- What about Paul's point of view?

Sharon is obviously committed to bringing up the child herself, and Paul has made it clear that he does not want any responsibility as a father.

However, Sharon would like her child to know his father and finds Paul's lack of interest very hurtful.

Dorret and Tony

Dorret and her partner Tony separated over three years ago, when he left the home to have another relationship. Dorret explains how she decided what to do about arrangements over the children.

Dorret

'I know he and the children had to keep in contact and I know that it had to be relaxed and okay. I did feel that it was important that their father saw them here at our home and that we showed the children that we could still get on together, by discussing things and all going out together. Even though it was hard for me, I knew it would get easier and I knew the pain of separation would subside.'

This is what they worked out:

'Tony comes to our house one Sunday and the children go to his the next. When he is here we have lunch together and we do something like visit a museum. Afterwards we eat together — he cooks or it's fish and chips which is the children's favourite. Then he baths them, puts them to bed and then goes.

'I feel our set-up is good, the children are happy enough and the visits are good. We still do things "as a family", and still have contact with his relatives. As far as discipline goes, he really backs me up, even on silly things like sitting properly at the table during a meal. He will repeat my request and tell the children to listen to what I say.'

But things are not ideal yet, and Dorret and Tony still have work to do ... as she explains:

'There is a lack of communication though. He never asks about things like how the children are getting on at school; it's always up to me to tell him. In fact, as I write I am planning to talk to him this Sunday. These days he doesn't stay on after putting the children to bed; he used to do that now and again and it gave us a chance to chat about things. I just really want to find out how he feels about the way things are three and a half years on.'

- What are the main reasons that Dorret and Tony's arrangements work well?
- Is she making it harder for herself by wanting them to do things 'as a family'?
- Would doing things 'as a family' confuse children about why their parents do not live together?

Shaheen and Nicholas

Shaheen and Nicholas have three children, Simon aged 17, Shaila aged 14 and Laurence aged 10. Shaheen left her husband after repeated domestic violence.

After staying in a refuge for a while, she was re-housed fifty miles away. The oldest child did not wish to see his father as he had often witnessed the results of his violence. The two younger ones missed their father and for the first year Shaheen took them to stay with him every weekend. Shaheen is now working full-time and is sharing a house with another woman who spends a great deal of time with the children.

Nicholas has since applied for custody of the two youngest children, saying that she is not fulfilling her role as a mother and that the two boys will be damaged with so much female company around.

Shaheen

'I refuse to be bullied by him. I have built up a life here from nothing. My children are content with what we have and we are stable and secure. He just can't stand to see me doing well. Knowing that my children are well balanced (I have worked very hard to make sure that the two youngest never hear me bad-mouthing their father) I feel they are free to make a choice about where they want to be.'

Nicholas

'My job has always been quite stressful and I suppose I just go over the top sometimes. I wouldn't touch the children though. I feel sure they will be better off with me. Boys especially need a male figure around.

'I have a good salary and a lovely house. I am putting money into bank accounts for each of the children. I also buy them a great deal. The older boy has been brainwashed into loyalty for Shaheen but the two youngest care about me and say they wouldn't mind living with me. But they won't hear a word against their mother or about what she's done.'

Simon (aged 17)

'I am very clear about my loyalties here. Dad was okay with us but very traditional. I can't forgive him for beating up my mum, though. Violence is wrong. I don't see he's got anything to make a fuss about. I would speak up for my mother any time. I don't really like to say it because he is my father, but if that's the model of being a man I'm supposed to follow, I can do without it.'

Shaila (aged 14)

'I'm really confused. Dad has always been good to us and I hated leaving my house and friends. I wasn't aware of some of the things going on — mum never let on. I don't want to have to choose between mum and dad.'

Laurence (aged 10)

'I didn't like leaving my home, dad and my friends. Dad has said that I can have everything I want if I come and live with him. He says it will be better for me and I need a father. I do miss him but mum is great. Dad says she can't do a good job with us. I don't really understand what is going on but I don't like them being unhappy.'

- What are Nicholas's grounds for wanting the children to live with him?
- Should the fact that he abused his wife, but not his children, be taken into account?
- Is Nicholas's claim that boys need a father around valid?

Guiding principles

We asked lone parents who read this chapter to tell us what principles guided their attitudes to and behaviour over parental responsibility. Here are some of them.

- Allow children to keep in contact with the other parent.
- Make the contact as relaxed as possible.
- Be honest with the children.
- Treat the other parent as well as possible and expect her/him to do likewise.
- Put the children's emotional security first.
- Talk to the children freely about the other parent, but do not run her/him down.
- Talk with the children about any problems that arise, and encourage them to do the same with you.
- Be aware that children's behaviour may differ according to their age, temperament and circumstances.

'Face yourself honestly and work out where the relationship went wrong. Work through the anger, bitterness, resentment, hatred and rejection, because as long as that stays with you, you can't grow.'

'Try and listen seriously to your children and draw out any fears or hopes they might have. For example, they may fear that their remaining parent will suddenly leave them, or hope that if you and your ex-partner are getting on well with each other you may get back together again. In this case, the situation should be explained, that being friendly is not the same as wanting to have a close relationship.'

'Children should know clearly that the separation is nothing to do with them, and that they will still be loved whatever happens. They need to know that it is the adults who don't get on well enough to live together any more.'

'The parent who doesn't live with the children should not try to buy the children's affections with gifts, food or money. This can be particularly hurtful if the other parent is less well-off and it gives the absent parent a "fairy godparent" image.'

Contacts

Families Need Fathers offers support over access and custody problems.
Ring London (081) 886 0970.

National Family Conciliation Council for information about conciliation services.
Ring 0793 514055.

Relate — National Marriage Guidance.
Ask Directory Enquiries or ring their national office on 0788 73241.

Stepfamily for advice and counselling for step families.
Ring London (071) 372 0844..

Solicitors Family Law Association will provide a list of solicitors in your area who subscribe to its code of practice. This is 'designed to encourage and assist parties to reach acceptable arrangements for the future in a positive and conciliatory way'.
Ring 0689 50227.

Where physical or sexual abuse is involved, the situation becomes more difficult. It is not easy to present the abusing parent in a positive light. It is important that children know that the abuse is wrong and the person should not have acted in that way. The children can then be told about any steps that the person is taking to make sure it does not happen again. Supervised access can help here.

Who else is involved?

Several lone parents who read this chapter mentioned the importance of children keeping up relationships with both sets of grandparents and other relatives, and with their friends. This can allow the children to see that the ending of a relationship does not mean they lose contact with the people they care for.

Stress and your life

'Whenever I've had a stressful patch I try to identify the cause and put it to one side. I go away and do something I'm really good at, then come back and tackle the problem again.'

'A lot of us live with stress as a normal fact of life, not a temporary thing. We often know we need to take stock, and the fact that we can't get it together to do that is a further cause of stress.'

Stress is not unusual. It is something everyone has to deal with. This chapter looks at some of the symptoms and causes of stress and how you might find solutions. It should help you deal with everyday stresses so that they do not build up to a crisis level. Occasionally, however, stress can become very extreme. Emergency or crisis situations, chronic depression, illness and addiction are beyond the scope of this book. If you are facing problems like these it would be a good idea to seek specialist advice. You will find some suggestions for people to contact at the end of this chapter.

What is stress?

Stress is physical or emotional pressure, brought about by your relationships and daily life. Stress can be positive; it keeps you on your toes, pushes you to change, stops you becoming stale and keeps you going. But too much stress can be negative. It stops you doing what you want to and it can cause discomfort, dissatisfaction, frustration, unhappiness and ill-health.

For some lone parents, too much stress is a permanent fact of life.

Recognising signs of stress in yourself

Particular events can cause or add to stress. Events like moving house, having a baby, changing jobs, or a child leaving home can be stressful for everyone. But lone parents often face these events on top of the stress caused by separation, divorce, or the death of a partner.

Add to this the discrimination faced by lone parents, by black people and other ethnic minorities and by people with disabilities, and you may wonder how some lone parents survive. But they do, and knowing what helps them may help you too.

Caring for yourself may not come easily. You may be so used to putting other people's needs first and making superhuman demands on yourself that you will not let yourself acknowledge when you are under stress, because you think it would be an admission of failure. But looking after yourself is the best thing you can do for others, as well as for yourself, because unless you are in good physical and mental health, you will find it harder to cope.

You may not always recognise when you are under stress. Some of the main symptoms of stress are listed below. These describe how you might be feeling, or behaving, as a result of stress. Read the list and tick any signs of stress that you recognise in your life. Doing this with other adults who know you well, or with your children, may give you useful feedback on how others see you. Sometimes other people may recognise the stress you are under and can help you to change.

Recognising stress

❑ There's a weight on my mind all the time.

❑ I don't seem to have any time for myself.

❑ I feel really 'on edge' most of the time.

❑ I find it easy to burst into tears.

❑ I'm shouting at the kids all the time.

❑ I'm irritable with friends and work colleagues.

❑ I'm eating too much.

❑ I don't look forward to the day ahead.

❑ I'm run down: I keep getting colds and bugs, and can't shake them off.

❑ I have to be doing something all the time, and my body and brain won't stop buzzing.

❑ I keep neglecting and forgetting important things.

❑ I need to sleep all the time.

❑ I'm relying on alcohol/tobacco/other drugs for comfort and escape.

❑ I can't work up any energy or enthusiasm.

❑ I can't sleep at night.

❑ I'm getting frequent headaches.

❑ I'm not giving the children enough attention.

❑ I feel guilty that I'm not a good parent.

❑ I'm spending too much money.

❑ I'm neglecting my appearance.

Whoever you are, you will probably have ticked some of these potential stress signs. Many of them are quite normal occurrences in themselves, such as overeating once in a while or the occasional sleepless night. It is when they start happening more frequently than usual and you do not feel good in yourself, that you need to take stock, find out what is causing you stress, and try to change it.

Causes of stress

Below we have given some examples of the things that are likely to make your life stressful. Some of them may be permanently present in your life — for example, inequality, lack of money, ill-health or housing problems. This chapter is unlikely to help you change these circumstances, but other parts of the book may help you begin to plan long-term changes. Other things that cause you stress may be temporary, so that you feel you have a better chance of changing them.

Look at the examples below and pick out the ones that are causing stress for you at the moment. Add any others in the spaces provided.

Identifying causes ... and dealing with them

The chart on the next page may help you to identify stress in your life.

For each of the four areas listed, first describe anything that is causing you stress. Next, write down how this makes you feel, then what you do when faced with this situation. Lastly, put down your ideas about how you could tackle the situation and deal with it differently. On page 50 there is an example of how one parent used the chart.

What causes stress?

- ❏ other people's attitudes to lone parents
- ❏ inequality
- ❏ prejudice
- ❏ environment
- ❏ too much change

- ❏ discrimination
- ❏ disability
- ❏ abuse
- ❏ feeling neglected by others
- ❏ too much responsibility for others

- ❏ unhappy relationships
- ❏ dislike of self
- ❏ difficulties with ex-partner
- ❏ children ill
- ❏ children playing up

- ❏ decision-making alone
- ❏ feeling bereaved
- ❏ children unhappy
- ❏ dislike your job
- ❏ demanding job

- ❏ housing problems
- ❏ lack of money
- ❏ isolation
- ❏ ill-health
- ❏ inadequate childcare provision

- ❏
- ❏
- ❏
- ❏
- ❏

1 Work and study

Situation | How you feel | Reactions | Solutions

2 Family relationships

Situation | How you feel | Reactions | Solutions

3 Personal and social

Situation | How you feel | Reactions | Solutions

4 Leisure and exercise

Situation | How you feel | Reactions | Solutions

Here are four possible ways of dealing with causes of stress:

■ Tackle the problem that causes the stress.

This can be by challenging, protesting, telling other people how you feel, talking it over, asking for help or taking some other practical action. However, this means you have to be prepared to get to the root of the problem rather than just deal with the stress it causes. For example, you may be stressed because you feel you are being taken for granted by your children. You need to deal with that rather than just complaining that they are not pulling their weight.

■ Ignore the problem, or avoid it and therefore avoid the stress.

If you know that seeing an ex-partner is going to be stressful, can you arrange ways of not having to see her or him? If the situation becomes intolerable you can leave it on a temporary or permanent basis. Turning your back on a problem *is* okay, but if you know that putting it off will eventually cause a build-up of other stresses, it might be better to tackle the problem head-on.

■ Change your attitude to the problem so that it no longer worries you and causes you stress.

Putting up with the situation and learning not to resent it really can be a solution. If you decide that you can cope with things as they are, or that doing something about them would be more stressful than letting them be, then you have to adjust and change your priorities. For example, you may be prepared to put up with poor housing because it is cheaper than any alternative, or because you know you will be moving in a year's time.

■ Learn to control or reduce the stress caused by the problem.

You could do this through exercise, relaxation, meditation, yoga or massage, or in other ways, depending on the type of stress and what you prefer to do. Talking to others in a similar position, joining a self-help group, or having good friends to call on, can all reduce stress.

Try to summarise what you have learned about yourself from producing the chart, and the main changes you have decided to try. Bridget's account of the stresses in her life and how she tackled them follow below.

Bridget's story

'I had to have a major operation and had only been home from hospital for one week when I was diagnosed as having a long-term illness which is not fatal but which cannot be cured.

'For five years I had been progressively improving our situation as a one parent family. For two years we lived on state benefit. When my youngest child started school I got a part-time job and gradually increased the hours and earnings until I was at the planning stage of buying our council house and considering driving lessons to increase both my earning capacity and complete independence from the State. I thought I'd made it, and suddenly there I was unable to go to work and learning that, even after recovery from the operation, I would find it hard to care for myself, never mind the children. My daughter had exams looming up.

'I became very concerned. How were we going to cope financially? How would we manage with day-to-day living? How could I bring up two children alone if it was taking an hour to dress myself in the mornings?

'There was no support offered from my ex-husband, just when his children needed him most. My own relationship with my boyfriend ended. I felt I'd lost everything, even my freedom, as I am almost housebound. I became irritable, anxious, angry because I felt robbed of all I'd worked hard to achieve.'

This is how Bridget filled in her chart:

1 Work and study

Situation Illness mean't I couldn't hold down my job

How you felt Anxious, irritable, angry, robbed

Reactions Crying a lot, short-tempered, tired

Solution Contacted work and DHSS.

2 Family relationships

Situation Relationship with boyfriend ended. No support from my 'ex'.

How you felt Panic. Felt I'd lost everything

Reactions Smoking, snapped at the kids.

Solution I let go of the past

3 Personal and social

Situation Worry about how day-to-day jobs would get done.

How you felt Anxious, trapped

Reactions Neglected my appearance. Wouldn't talk to friends.

Solution Contacted Gingerbread and a home-help service.

4 Leisure and exercise

Situation Would I ever have energy again.

How you felt Cheated.

Reaction Wringing my hands.

Solution Learned to manage the illness.

Bridget's main causes of stress can be summarised as:

- her health
- financial
- practical problems of managing a household and bringing up two children alone while disabled
- lack of support from partner and ex-partner
- too many changes to cope with at once.

These were her solutions:

1 *'I contacted my employers and explained my situation. They told me how long I would be entitled to statutory sick pay and also kept my job open for a while in case of recovery. This gave me time to work on my finances.'*

2 *'I contacted the DSS for leaflets and information on sickness and invalidity benefits.'*

3 *'I contacted an association for people with my illness, and they sent me more information on benefits and put me in touch with other people in a similar situation. They also gave guidelines on how to manage this illness.'*

4 *'I applied for and got a home-help for three two-hour sessions per week. Great difference.'*

5 *'I contacted my friends in Gingerbread and they helped me and still do. They take the children out for a few hours so that I can rest and the children can have a break from me. They keep me in touch with the local group now that I can't attend meetings. They gave me lifts to the doctor's on days when I had no statutory help. Someone will cook a meal now and then or simply visit me or telephone. Tremendous!'*

6 *'I let go of the past. Let go the old relationship. Let go of the old dreams and started counting my blessings. I made a conscious decision to take charge of my own health wherever possible and to do whatever it took to improve it in any way. I concentrate on health and happiness, for myself and my children. I listen to other people's worries too, it keeps life in proportion.'*

'My children and I are now a lot happier and more able to adjust to our situation. They like me being at home and having more time with them. I am watching them grow in confidence since they now expect me to do less for them and they take more responsibility for themselves. I may be less mobile but I'm still here to guide them.'

Bridget's story illustrates how stressful events can turn a life upside down, but that it is possible to readjust, find the positive things in your life, and build on these.

Other guidelines that can help deal with stress or prevent it occurring are listed on the next page.

Guidelines

- **Be realistic** about how much you can cope with at a time and put aside the things that can wait or are not really important. Read the *Organising your time* chapter (page 53).

- **Don't bottle things up**. When a problem starts to get you down, discuss it with someone whose judgment you trust. Read *Getting help and support* (page 25).

- **Learn to relax**. There are plenty of useful books on relaxation in libraries and shops as well as classes in many centres.

- **Make time** to do things you really enjoy and to develop new skills. This will give you more confidence and energy to cope with unavoidable pressures. Activities like gardening, reading library books, writing and voluntary work can cost very little.

- **Take a break**. When you feel that you are going round in circles with a problem, stop and do something else for a while. Even a change of routine can help.

- **Remember the value of exercise**. As well as helping you to keep fit, it is a good way to work off your tensions. You do not have to attend formal classes. Walking is excellent exercise.

- **Get enough sleep**. Do not skimp on sleep which you need, but on the other hand do not worry if you miss out on sleep sometimes, as long as you are feeling well.

- **Eat sensibly**. Don't neglect the kind of food needed for good health. Even if you have very little money to spare you may still have time to hunt around and make the most of what you can afford.

- **Yoga** helps deal with stress by focusing the mind, keeping the body physically active and using relaxation techniques. Many adult education centres run daytime and evening yoga classes.

- **Massage** is a good way of getting rid of body tension; you can teach yourself from books and get someone to learn with you.

We asked lone parents to give us their solutions for dealing with symptoms of stress. Here are some of their ideas:

'Make plans for yourself — places to go, people to see, holidays, things that please you.'

'Treat yourself — if only to a bar of chocolate.'

'When I got really worried about how I was going to cope, I talked things over with one of my friends. I was surprised at how much better it made me feel — even though the problems were still there.'

'Do some vigorous activity — dig the garden, clean the windows.'

'Meditation has helped me prevent stress from happening.'

'I cuddle the children.'

'I rely a lot on my friends in Gingerbread to help — they've all been through it too.'

'When angry, I throw potatoes at the back wall!'

Contacts

British Association for Counselling for information about local counselling services. Ring 0788 78328/9.

Samaritans. Look under Samaritans in the phone book or ask Directory Enquiries.

National Association of Young People's Counselling and Advisory Services for information about counselling for under 25s. Ring 0533 471200 ext 341 or 558763.

7 Organising your time

'Looking after three children under 5 years is very time-consuming, but occasionally I will "put my foot down" and make time to do something I want to do, whether it be reading, or having a friend round or whatever. My own needs usually take second place but at least I make sure I get enough sleep. My form of exercise is running about making sure all three are not doing anything they shouldn't. At the moment, I feel that if I have enough sleep I can cope.'

'I believe you can always make the time to do the things you want to do if you are flexible enough in your routine.'

Many people, not just lone parents, find that they cannot do the things they want to do, either because they do not have enough time or because other things always seem more important and have to be done first. Others find they have too much time on their hands and do not know what to do with it.

This chapter shows you a way of organising your time by looking at what you do and how you do it, and then deciding where you want to make changes in the way you use your time.

If your life is busy and hectic you need to work out how to make time for yourself. Or, if you feel you have too much time on your hands, you may need to think about different ways of using it.

To organise your time, you will need to:

● work out what really happens to your time
● decide what is most important to you
● work out how much energy you have
● know where your support lies.

Keeping a time diary

A good way of finding out what happens to your time is to keep a 'time diary'. In this you keep a record of everything you do throughout a day or a week, and see how much time it takes you. After that, you look to see where time could be saved, or used better, by changing things around or by not doing certain things.

Choose a couple of 'typical' days. You could pick a weekday and a Saturday or Sunday, or one day when you are working away from home and one when you are not. During the day, keep a note of how you are spending your time, like 'Teresa's day'. Then look back over what you have done and how long it took to do different things.

Work out which bits of your days are spent on activities that you cannot easily change, or that you need to carry out to stay fit and well. These activities are likely to include shopping, eating, sleeping, taking exercise, earning money, studying and looking after your children. They make up time that is 'fixed' for you and is not likely to change.

The time you have left is time you can be flexible with. This is the time you have for yourself, your home, your social life and for all the other things you want to do. When you look at your account, note down which activities you would like to spend more time on and which you would rather spend less on.

Teresa's day

- **'6.30 am** *Woke up — saw the time and went back to sleep.*

- **7 am** *Woke up and remembered that I had promised myself to get up at 6.30 am and write an essay for college — started it.*

- **7.10 am** *Was disturbed by tousled daughter (aged 5) carrying snakes and ladders, looking hopeful.*

- **7.45 am** *Finished second game which (guilt) had been initiated by me as a good excuse for not having to do the essay.*

- **8 am** *Breakfast — interrupted by me rushing about trying to do some overdue housework.*

- **8.30 am** *Mad rush to get daughter dressed, do hair, teeth, pack school bag, find urgent books, answer urgent queries, then do it all again — for me this time (plus make-up).*

- **9.05 am** *Daughter, bicycle, lots of bags (swimming lesson as well today) and I struggle up hill. Resist beseeching voice asking me to show her how to hop-scotch properly.*

- **9.20 am** *Arrive at school, hang things up on pegs, search for peg name-tag which seems to be very important to my daughter, get talked into reading a story, fail to get several weak jokes.*

- **9.30 am** *Rush off to college.*

- **4.30 pm** *Rush back from college — a million and one necessary things to do in my head. Plan to do them all this evening — realise I can't as half of them involve post office, or have to be done in office hours (getting new childminders' list from social services, etc).*

- **5 pm** *Arrive at childminder's. All good intentions go out of window. 45 minutes and two cups of coffee and a good chat later, just make it to shop before it closes, to buy tea. Deep freezer in shop uninspiring and full of*

things which I am sure I have heard are bad for children. Am persuaded to buy oven chips and turkey steaks. Horrified by price — must try to shop consistently and in a more organised fashion at weekends. I cannot afford corner shop prices.

- **6 pm** *Arrive home. Neighbours come over. I breathe a sigh of relief — Sally complains.*

- **6.30 pm** *Tea on table and water on floor. I have had a helper washing the plates.*

- **6.35 pm** *Telephone rings.*

- **6.40 pm** *Telephone rings again.*

- **7 pm** *Finish eating and wonder if I dare take the risk of swearing at next caller. Decide not to — it might be my mother. Telephone doesn't ring again.*

- **7.30 pm** *Sally bathed, brushed (teeth and hair) and unable to make up her mind as to which of two stories to have. Read both.*

- **8 pm** *Daughter in bed and asleep. I look at my desk then burrow into the newspaper instead.*

- **8.45 pm** *Decide to do my essay but end up doing this account instead.*

- **10.45 pm** *Too tired to work any more. Promise myself to get up at 6.30 and do the essay tomorrow.'*

'Looking at this account, I seem to spend my time rushing around trying to fit everything in and feeling guilty that I haven't managed to do everything I think I should have done. I was glad to see that spending time with Sally, relaxing at the childminder's and reading the newspaper took priority over work. They're the things that keep me sane. If I could find a few hours each week I could probably do all the "office" jobs. Perhaps I could take a long lunch or miss the occasional course session.'

Too much time on your hands?

Hetty made a record of her day:

> **'8 o'clock.** *Get up — I am always woken up by Karl — never wake up on my own. I get Karl out of his cot, give him a drink and a biscuit. I go back to bed and doze. I feel as though I have been intruded upon by being woken and this makes me bad tempered. About one hour later I get up and make some breakfast (I have a big eating problem as I tend to binge, mainly out of anger, frustration and boredom). The day then seems to stretch out in front of me with nothing much to do but visit the DSS.*
>
> *'I then clean up and wash and get dressed which usually takes me until midday. Karl goes to sleep then and I just sit and read or watch television or write this. I have a coffee and a biscuit and wait for Karl — then go out for a walk — then back at 4 pm to cook dinner. Dad comes about 5 pm. Sometimes I go swimming at about 6 pm. I come back about 7.30 pm, get Karl to bed and watch television or a friend comes round. I go out about once a week.'*

Hetty has time to spend on recreational activities and can be quite flexible with her time, because she is not spending time earning money or looking for work. She is clearly not happy with her situation and looks forward to changes:

'It's not all bad though. I hope to go back to work when Karl goes to school. I was a secretary with a very good job.'

And in the meanwhile she has opportunities to make friends, and can find time to do things like making clothes, and to train ready for going back to work.

For Hetty, it is a question of her using her time differently in order to ease the frustration and boredom she feels.

If, like Hetty, you have difficulty filling your days and would like some ideas about new things to do, you could read the chapters on *Making changes* (page 65), and *Getting help and support* (page 25). The chapter on *Stress and your life* may also help (page 45).

How much time is 'enough' for your children?

In some ways, time spent with your children should be in the 'fixed time' category, and you may wish to count it as such. But there is no agreement about how much time parents ought to spend with their children. A parent could spend the whole day in the company of her/his children, and hardly speak to them at all, or their time together might be limited but they could enjoy themselves and do things together.

The answer is to find something that feels satisfying for you. If you are spending more time than you want to with your children, use your time diary to identify where you could make cuts, bring extra people in to support you or find childcare. If you want to spend more time with them, the diary should help you to see where you could make time.

How much can children do?

In Britain, families have traditionally seen childhood as a period when children are shielded from responsibility and do not have to take part in day-to-day tasks and household routines. This means that parents may feel guilty about asking their children to do their share of tasks, or may feel the children are not capable of doing them. Women have traditionally been expected to do everything, with some 'help' from the rest of the family — but the responsibility for the housework is still theirs. Ideally, everyone should see it as a shared responsibility. It also provides an opportunity for you to spend time with your children without feeling that this takes you away from things that have to be done.

Try this quiz. Your replies will depend on the age of your children, but there are still 'children' of 18 who live at home and have never cooked a meal or done the washing or ironing in their lives!

Which of the following do your children do?

- ❏ Wake themselves up in the morning.
- ❏ Get dressed by themselves.
- ❏ Make their own packed lunches (the night before if necessary).

- ❏ Make their beds.
- ❏ Clear away their toys, equipment, clothes.
- ❏ Put dirty clothes in a basket/machine.
- ❏ Care for younger sisters and brothers.

- ❏ Cook a meal.
- ❏ Check the oil, water, tyres on a car.
- ❏ Sweep/wash/vacuum the floors.
- ❏ Put washing through the machine and drier.

- ❏ Iron clothes.
- ❏ Make a shopping list.
- ❏ Do the shopping.
- ❏ Buy/choose their own clothes.

Now look at the list again. For any item that you have not ticked, ask yourself whether your children could do this for themselves. If the answer is still no, would you be able to teach them how?

Making plans

When you have collected the information about how you spend your weekdays and weekends and decided what you would like to spend more, or less, time on, you can help yourself put these decisions into practice by writing your ideas down and working out how you could carry them out.

First, write down things you would like to change soon. For example, you may want to spend less time cooking and more with the children. This may mean buying more prepared foods, or doing more cooking at the weekend or when the children are not around. You may also want to increase the time you have left for relaxing or having fun, or change the way you use this time.

You may also have long-term plans for how you want to spend your time. These could involve changes in the 'fixed time' categories — getting or changing a job, working part-time, working from home, taking up a new hobby or going to college. All will involve setting new ways of organising your time.

I would like to change these things soon:

Ways I might make the change:

Use the following space to set down some longer-term priorities, and what this might mean for you. For example, Hetty was looking forward to returning to work once Karl was at school. She could be planning for this now by building up her contacts so that she would be able to get after-school (and before-school) care if necessary. She could also look at retraining or refresher courses to update her skills. If money is short, she could look at ways of earning at home or part-time.

I would like to change these things in the future:

Ways I might make the change:

Energy level

It may be stating the obvious, but in order to make changes you have got to want them to happen. This means being prepared to overcome obstacles, and not finding excuses which will stop you from making changes. Many of the lone parents who wrote to us had achieved more than they ever thought possible, and each achievement had brought new energy and enthusiasm. If you feel too fed up to start getting organised, look at the chapters *Stress and your life* (page 45) and *Making changes* (page 65).

If you are feeling tired and drained of energy, then you may be neglecting your health and need to think about taking more care of yourself.

Support

Making changes is not always easy and it will help if you can share any difficulties with someone else. Other lone parents were probably once in the same situation as you. Their support can give you new energy, new ideas and enthusiasm. Read the chapters *Getting help and support* (page 25) and on *Meeting other lone parents* (page 89).

8 Making time for yourself

'I use my spare time for reading and writing letters. I look forward to my bath; it's the only time I have to myself. I put in loads of bubble bath, take a book and stay there for 30-40 minutes.'

'When the children are in bed it is my time, which I use to catch up on serials that I have videotaped, or generally do things to suit the mood I'm in.'

You have a right to time of your own, when you can choose what you want to do, or when you can feel you do not have to do anything at all. This is part of taking care of yourself, and it will help you to care more effectively for your children and the other people who matter to you.

Although time for yourself may include being with your children, in this chapter it means time when you do not have to be with them unless you want to be.

Two lone parents who wrote to us show just how important 'their' time was to them, and also how they had to plan for it and use it to do something that pleased and benefited them.

Debbie

'I can't wait for my break. I'm glad I kept my cool in the early days and worked towards good access arrangements. He's not really keen, but I was determined a year ago that my "ex" was going to see the children. It was on my terms, for a weekend, every other weekend, from Friday evening until Sunday tea-time. It is the only thing that keeps me sane these days. The freedom is unbelievable, to get up and get out in ten minutes. To be in the house for two hours and for it still to look the same, not wrecked. It also gives me time for activities like swimming, watching football and ice skating.'

Morag

'Spare time is usually alternate weekends — but not regularly — when the children visit my parents. These days, since I became ill, it takes all my energy to deal with basics. Occasionally I'll go to family or friends for lunch or tea, for a change. I enjoy lazing in the bath for as long as I like without being needed by the children. At night if I'm alone, I can choose a TV programme to watch without having to consider whether it's suitable viewing for them. My own time before going to bed will be spent reading a book or doing a crossword to stop the brain "going to seed".

'I use other spare time to go at my own pace, catching up on jobs that would be difficult with the children about. Some weekends we spend with other one parent families, perhaps on a day trip or at a barbecue, with Gingerbread. Since I cannot get to Gingerbread meetings and some socials (which I did a lot for five years) due to illness, I spend some of my spare time catching up on group news via the telephone, or else I'll ring my sister, and have a long chat with her.'

When did you last have time for yourself?

Make a note of when you last had time that you could really say was yours, when you felt no pressure to do anything for anyone else. It could be time you spent alone in your home, or in someone else's, or it could be time when you were right away from where you live.

Make a note of what you did with the time.

If you cannot remember the last time you were able to plan and do something just for yourself, you should take seriously your need for time off and try to organise something soon.

Some lone parents told us about their recent time off:

Jenny

'My parents treated my son to a four day school trip. I dreaded it at first, thinking I'd be very lonely but found it okay really — thanks to friends with whom I went out twice. The evenings were relaxing but no early start between six and seven in the morning was absolute heaven!'

Dorcie

'Two weeks ago was my birthday. My sister had the children to sleep at her house, so I was able to have a leisurely tea on my own. I had a long bath without having to listen to the children fighting and got ready to go out without having to avoid the youngest seeing me dressed up! I then went out for a drink with some friends, went back to one of their homes and ordered pizzas. I got home about two in the morning, and had a long lie-in the next day.'

Peter

'Two months ago, an old school friend invited Danielle and me to stay with them for a week. One day they took Danielle out and I had the day to myself. I spent the morning shopping, had lunch in a wonderful cheap cafe and read a magazine all the way through: it was wonderful. In the afternoon I sat in my friend's garden, slept for a couple of hours, then had a shower and — something I never enjoy doing at home — baked some biscuits. The week was great but that day made such a difference to my sense of freedom.'

Planning time for yourself

For many people, time off does not just happen. It has to be planned in advance. This means:

- putting yourself first for a change
- being determined that time off has priority over everything else, just for a while
- making it clear to children, friends, family, or ex-partner that your time off is important
- not feeling guilty
- making practical arrangements for childcare.

You may not be used to caring for yourself. You may feel guilty about it, and others may make you feel guilty, particularly if you are a woman. You must believe that you deserve some time of your own.

How would you finish these sentences?

I deserve to have time to myself because ...

I want my children to understand that having time to myself is important because ...

When I have time to myself I feel ...

If you are convinced of your right to time for yourself, think about how you can find this time. Look through your diary or a calendar and try these suggestions.

1 Find when you could give yourself some time away from your responsibilities. It may be when someone is coming to stay, when the children are away, or simply a time when you have not yet planned to do anything.

2 Decide what you would ideally like to do with the time: stay at home, see a film, visit friends, read a book, do nothing, go shopping, go fishing, go somewhere by bus or train.

3 Think about the typical things that are most likely to stop you from taking this time off. For example, *'I'd like to have two hours to myself on Thursday night but the children will probably want help with their homework'*, or, *'I bet if I plan to go out on Saturday my parents will let me down ...'*

4 Work out which of these obstacles are genuine problems which can be dealt with — like getting a babysitter — and which ones are just excuses because you are not used to having time off, or because you feel guilty about leaving the children. For example:

'I'm sure my ex-wife won't turn up on time' could be planned for by impressing on her that you have to go out at a certain time, then having a fall-back plan that the children can wait with friends or someone will come and sit with them until she arrives.

'I don't have the money to go anywhere.' Many lone parents have found cheap or free ways of spending time — doing voluntary work which pays travel expenses; window shopping; reading in the local library; jumble or car boot sales; local parks; having a coffee with a friend.

'I feel guilty leaving the children with a babysitter or relatives' is an understandable feeling, but one that you need to challenge: you are just as entitled to time off as anyone else and the children will often get something out of being with other adults.

Easy to say, but hard to do

If you are still finding it hard to plan time for yourself, it may be useful to think about recent occasions when you really wished you could have time off.

'Sometimes I get home from work absolutely exhausted. It would be ideal if I could have a shower and go straight to bed, instead of having to cook tea for the children and generally seeing to them first.'

'Whenever I am busy at work and have to bring work home, I always seem to have more to do for the family as well — like birthday parties to organise or the children needing more attention for various reasons. Consequently I end up going to bed about 1 am, and then I'm tired the following day.'

By looking at the circumstances surrounding these times, you may be able to plan so that you do get time off in the future. If you plan to have a little time for yourself each day, the need to have full days or weekends off should not be so great.

'I had one weekend free. The children were with me. They were playing. I was going to tackle the garden. We got a call to go and see my ex-partner because his father was suddenly found to be terminally ill. My solution? Not to rely so much on any particular day off and to plan ahead for more free time so that one lost day isn't so important.'

'During the summer school holidays I have to work. My sister has the children for me, so I feel I can't ask her any more than is necessary. Consequently I am either working or have the children with me. Roll on September, when I can have a day off without the children! If there were all-day play schemes in this area, it would help.'

These examples may have reminded you of other situations. What would have been a solution for you?

Finding patterns

Are there any situations that make it more likely that you will need time for yourself? For example, if the children are upset, if you have not seen your best friend for a couple of days, if work is demanding. What would help?

■ Help with childcare

Babysitters and daytime childcare usually cost money, which is a problem for many lone parents. Gingerbread groups may run babysitting schemes or members themselves may have older children who can babysit. Some childminders are prepared to take children part-time on a regular basis. Both childminders and social services departments are often sympathetic to the needs of lone parents. Some local authorities also offer childminding subsidies, and adult education centres, colleges, recreation and shopping centres may have creches.

Find out whether there are any after-school childcare services available (ask at local schools or at the council offices). These are usually inexpensive, as are holiday play schemes.

Building up a group of friends who will occasionally share childcare with you can give all of you a break. Many of the lone parents who wrote to us had arrangements with ex-partners, older children, relatives or friends that allowed them time for themselves. They also made good use of playgroup or nursery facilities.

'While my daughter is at playgroup I either read, do a tapestry, have a keyboard lesson, visit a friend or do absolutely nothing.'

'Most Sunday evenings I go out at about 9.30 pm, to a local pub, with about four others from Gingerbread. My eldest son usually looks after the rest of the children, but as he is about to go into the army, I will soon need a babysitter.'

'I take my youngest to nursery at 12.45 pm, until 3.00 pm. That gives me two hours to myself — bliss! I visit friends, do housework or read or bake biscuits and cakes.'

■ Time off from regular routines

Just taking a break from what you normally do can be 'time off'. It can give you energy to tackle jobs you find less attractive.

■ Taking on paid or voluntary work

This can provide new interests and a new purpose, as well as bringing in money. If you can choose how much work you do and it is not too stressful, it can be classed as 'time for yourself'. You may, however, find that the availability of free or cheap childcare limits the things you can do.

■ Someone to do things with

If you involve other people, they can help you to think about yourself. If you make arrangements to do pleasurable things with others, it is harder to cancel or change your mind.

■ Determination and confidence

Sometimes it is easier to feel sorry for yourself than to take a risk and make changes. Even if you know why you deserve time for yourself, you may lack the will or confidence to take action. Telling other people your plans can be helpful.

If you find you cannot get up the enthusiasm to do things, or you feel unable to make choices, it may help to read the chapters on *'Getting help and support'* (page 25) and *'Meeting other lone parents'* (page 89).

9 Making changes

'I would like more hours in the day to do everything I want to. I want to return to paid employment. I want to pass my driving test, find time to study ... '

'Becoming a lone parent removed a lot of stress. I got employment through voluntary work, gained confidence and independence. I made new relationships, learned new skills and took courses. Now ill-health means I have a whole new set of changes to make. These will take some achieving — rather like entering a marathon, for that is what life has become.'

Change may be something you feel in control of, or something that is forced upon you. Or you may feel you need to make changes in your life but are not sure what to do, or how.

Elsewhere in this book we look at relationships and changes to your social life. This chapter concentrates on employment, education, training and developing new skills. All these areas involve personal change and you will find this chapter useful even if you are not looking for a paid job.

What is your story so far?

Spend a few minutes, perhaps with a friend, thinking about and writing down ways in which your life has changed in the last few years.

For example:

'Rebuilding my life. Being able to find work when my youngest child began school full-time.'

'I helped start up a residents' action group, and have learned that with a "guiding hand" I can achieve many things that at first seemed impossible.'

'The major change in the last few years has been getting divorced. Since my divorce I have become a more independent, capable and happier person. I will attempt new things now, even if I do them badly; previously I would never have attempted anything new for fear of being "put down".'

'During the last year I have had part-time jobs — running a discussion group and teaching basic typing — which have allowed me to recover my confidence and self-esteem.'

There may have been changes in your life in some of these areas:

- getting a job
- removing stress
- giving up waged work
- gaining confidence
- becoming more independent

- learning new skills
- doing voluntary work
- making new relationships
- training or re-training
- learning for its own sake

- getting a qualification
- going on a course
- finding out about yourself
- setting up in business
- taking day or evening classes.

Some of the lone parents who replied to our questionnaire gave details of changes they had made:

'My life has taken a new direction and I feel I am doing some good for other people — I do voluntary work as a welfare officer for ex-army families. My job is as a home care assistant, taken up after my marriage breakup. People often "cry on my shoulder" and ask for advice.'

'I felt very sorry for myself for ages, thinking nobody would want to employ someone disabled like me. The turning point came for me eight years ago, when the (then) Greater London Council set up and supported local employment projects for disabled people. I got training in book-keeping and financial accounting and learned to use a computer. I now run a home-based financial consultancy service, particularly for charities and community groups.'

'I have one day a week to myself when I do voluntary work with older people. Sometimes children need a break from you as much as you do from them.'

'I was widowed in 1978, worked nights for eighteen months with help from a childminder. Then I was made redundant, but I found my three children much happier, so I decided not to seek work actively and lived on Supplementary Benefit for seven years. I had a child (now aged 4) from an unsuccessful relationship and have joint custody. Am working nightshifts again.'

'I have done several courses at evening classes and during the day (with childcare facilities). I joined Gingerbread four years ago — very shy I might add — but overcame that and am now the chairperson. I am now training for the local Gingerbread office one day a week and enjoy that.'

'I was persuaded to join the local playgroup and found there were other lone parents and plenty of people to care about me. I'm thinking of becoming a playgroup leader.'

'When my daughter began infant school, I started going to college, and in February I shall begin an Arts course with the Open University.'

Now spend a few minutes thinking what you would like the next part of your story to be. If you feel your aim might be hard to achieve, think what the first step towards it might be. You could make this your first goal. You can use this space to make a note of your goal.

These are some of the goals that some of the lone parents we consulted set themselves.

'I want to have someone caring, cheerful and responsible to live with us as part of the family.'

'Better organised at home. Greater support in my present circumstances and eventual return to fitness and independence.'

'I want to return to work. The first step will be to find out what training opportunities are available.'

'I'm registering as a childminder in the next few months. I've been elected on to my local Gingerbread Committee. I hope my new relationship remains fulfilling.'

'I would like to take a course in youth training. I would like to learn more about book-keeping and accounting.'

Looking at your situation

Being a lone parent provides new opportunities for people to make changes. To make successful changes, or to cope with changes that have occurred, you may need time, money, support or motivation. These four are linked, but it can help to think about each of them separately.

■ Time

You need time to make changes. If you cannot stop and think things through, you may rush into decisions that you later regret.

Bringing up children alone can be very time-consuming. Many lone parents wonder whether they will ever get enough uninterrupted time just to sit and relax for ten minutes. But for some people, becoming a lone parent creates more time. Evenings and weekends can be free to spend with the children — and if you have access arrangements, or relatives and friends nearby, there can be times without the children as well.

> ● Have you got time to yourself to take stock?
> ● If not, can you see how you can make time for this? The chapter *Organising your time* (page 53) may help you.

■ Money

Lack of money may be forcing change on you, or stopping you from making the changes you want. Check up on your rights to benefits. You may not be claiming all you are entitled to. Check your tax position too. If you are paying more tax than you should you could get a refund. If you are able to manage on the money that comes in — whether from pensions, benefits, insurance, maintenance, wages or grants — then you have some choice over what you do with your time. You might be able to get grants, loans, wages or your expenses paid for new things you take on.

'One big obstacle for people trying to get off benefits is being able to earn enough to be truly independent. It took me five years to achieve this. I just kept increasing my earning capacity a little at a time. Coupled with free child care, I was able to increase the hours I worked. Eventually I was able to look for a full-time job and pay for after-school childcare.'

■ Support

Personal support is very important. It is easier to face changes and meet new challenges if you know there are people around who will encourage you and back you up. Lone parents (like everyone else) need to build up a group of friends, relatives, neighbours and others they can call on for support. These are people who, in turn, must be able to call on you for support.

You also need practical support, for example, someone to look after the children while you go out to work or socialise, or people who can help you gain practical skills or tackle a big job.

You may not like to ask for help, especially if you feel you have to show that you can cope on your own. Sometimes support may not be forthcoming. Some people may envy your success or disapprove of your independence. Others may feel threatened. In these cases, you may need to turn to new people for personal support.

> ● Do you feel you have enough personal support? If not, look at the chapter *Getting help and support* (page 25). Lone parent groups can often provide support for people who cannot call on friends or family.

'Friendships are very important to me as I have no contact with my own family. Once the initial shock wore off I could motivate myself as I felt I had to get out and meet new people. Now I like to support others too.'

■ Motivation and energy

Starting something new takes energy as well as time. Sometimes the thought can be daunting — particularly if you are not confident that you will succeed. Often, though, getting started is the hardest part. Each step along the way your successes multiply and your motivation to succeed becomes stronger.

Try to break down the changes you want to make into smaller steps that you have a better chance of achieving. This can be particularly relevant if you have a disability which may mean that achieving what you want takes longer, no matter how motivated you are.

'Disability increases the amount of support needed to help with change. A highly motivated disabled person still needs great encouragement and practical support.'

- ● Do you feel ready to make changes?
- ● Are you excited by the changes you want to make? If not, read the chapters *On our own — and doing fine* (page 15) and *Getting help and support* (page 25).

Time, money, support and motivation are all linked. Change in one of these areas often leads to change in the others. If you are short of one or more of these, you may find it emerges along with the others.

For example, support from others can give you **motivation**:

'I really felt cheered up after my friend spent an evening with me; I got on the phone and sorted out my income tax.'

It can also help you earn or obtain **money**:

'My parents lent me £50, my babysitter gave me four free nights a month so I could take a refresher course and get on to the temporary register.'

If you feel motivated you can seek **support** and create the **time** you need to begin to make changes:

'I persuaded a friend to have the kids for a day and I spent it in the library looking for local organisations I could join, courses I could do, jobs I could apply for.'

'After I visited the debt counselling service, I was determined to claim every penny I was entitled to. Every week for two months I visited the library, read up about benefits, sent for forms and filled them in. I got a tax rebate which paid off my debt!'

What do you want to do?

Use this checklist to work out where you would like to make changes, and how soon you would like to make them. Tick the ones that apply to you and add any other changes of your own. If you do not feel ready to do this now, complete the *Strengths and skills* questionnaire on page 70 first.

Changes I would like to make	Soon	In the future
Find new pastimes/hobbies.	❏	❏
Learn a new practical skill, for example, car maintenance, hairdressing, word processing.	❏	❏
Learn something for its own sake/improve myself.	❏	❏
Get back into employment after bringing up the children.	❏	❏
Improve my job prospects for the future.	❏	❏
Take a course to help me get a job.	❏	❏
Change my job.	❏	❏
Do my current job better.	❏	❏
Get formal qualifications, for example City and Guilds.	❏	❏

When you have completed the checklist, make a list of all the changes you would like to make. Try to be as specific as possible — for example, if you know what hobbies you would like to take up, or if you know what qualifications you need, list them.

If your list is long, pick out your top three. Think about how achievable each one of them will be. Don't set yourself targets you cannot possibly reach; choose at least one thing that can be achieved quickly.

Strengths and skills

Use this questionnaire to help you work out what you like and are good at doing. You might learn a bit more about yourself and what you have achieved.

Interests
- What do you enjoy doing?
- What do you dislike doing, or find dull and boring?
- What work would you like to do if you had a free choice?

Talents and skills
- What are you good at doing now?
- What could you do well, with practice?
- What are you not good at doing?
- What do you find difficult to learn?
- Make a list of all your skills, from driving a car, storytelling, listening, cooking, to any unusual skills or advanced training you have.

Formal education
- What qualifications do you have? for example RSA, GCE, GCSE, City and Guilds.
- What courses or training have you taken since leaving school (or since entering Britain if you were not born in this country) ?

Paid or voluntary work experience
- What is your current or last job?
- What do you (did you) like and dislike about it?
- What bits do you (did you) do best, and why?
- What do you (did you) do least well, and why?
- What have you learned from the job to help you in the future (for example, practical skills, how to be more assertive, to be aware of discrimination, to sell yourself more)?

Paid or voluntary work?
- Do you have limits on your time that would affect what job you could do?
- Do you have any physical limitations that would affect the job you could do?
- Do you like lots of responsibility, or prefer to leave this to others?
- Do you prefer to work alone or as part of a team?
- Do you need to work to earn enough money to live on? Or can you work for expenses only?

Knowing what you are good at and what you enjoy doing should make you feel good about yourself.

'The questionnaire showed me that my life is quite full, my interests are varied and I have a few skills.'

'The questionnaire made me think about myself, and what I have achieved — even if I feel it's only a little. It made me think about what I can do to change things.'

If you are aiming to take on paid employment or change jobs then the questionnaire can help you choose work suited to you. If you are not looking for paid work, it may help you work out how you can use your talents to benefit others or to enjoy yourself.

You may find it difficult to list your skills and talents: many people find it difficult to 'boast' like this. If you cannot think of many, ask a friend to help you complete the list.

'It is quite difficult to see your own strengths and skills. They are often seen better by other people.'

Making an action plan

For each of the changes you have decided to make, set up an action plan.

1 Set a target for the change you want to make.

For example:
- I want to have a job in six months' time.
- I'd like to pass my driving test by April.
- I want to find somewhere I can do voluntary work for two months.

2 Work out the steps you need to take to reach the target.

For example, you might take the following steps if your aim is to get a job:
- decide what job I want to do next
- decide what new skills I need to get this job
- write down my work experience
- look at the newspapers for job adverts
- ask around for any local vacancies
- learn to use a typewriter or word processor
- practise writing applications.

3 Who do you need to contact? Who do you need to negotiate with?

For example:
- friends in work
- ex-partner
- parents
- library
- job centre
- tax office.

4 Work out what has to change in the following areas, and how:
- children
- ex-partner
- home management
- your friends
- your employer
- your finances
- childcare
- relatives
- your time schedule.

Obstacles to change

■ Your children

They may have taken you for granted, particularly if you are a woman. They may be jealous of the changes you are making. They may feel your changes mean less attention for them.

■ Your family

They may not support some of your decisions. Men may be discouraged from giving up paid work; women may be discouraged from taking work on, becoming independent or better qualified.

■ Your friends

Some may like you when you are vulnerable, and feel threatened when you show strength and purpose. Some may be jealous of your success, if you are doing things they would secretly like to do.

■ Your colleagues

Workmates may discourage you from applying for promotion, taking courses or training. They might see you as competing for jobs they want.

■ Yourself

Your own lack of self-esteem and confidence can be obstacles to change. You may have come to believe some of the outside world's prejudices, in which lone parents are seen as 'unable to cope', or black people as 'unskilled' or women as 'unable to do what men can do'. You may need other people's encouragement to help you get into a positive frame of mind.

■ Discrimination

Discrimination can crop up in education, workplaces or organisations. For example, the process of recruitment and selection of staff often discriminates against people with children, black people, women, disabled people, lesbians and gay men.

Lone parents, particularly women, may be asked questions about how they intend to care for their children, a question that would not be asked of a two parent family. Increasingly, it is seen as bad practice for potential employers to ask about marital status and childcare arrangements (unless the workplace offers childcare facilities to employees).

Being aware of discrimination and of the many forms it takes means you can recognise it when it happens and know that it is not your fault. You can also gather evidence to stand up for yourself and challenge bad work practices.

Contacts

Educational Guidance or **Advice Services** are available in many areas. Ask at the library or ring the Education Department of your city, borough or county council. The local **adult education service** should also be able to help you find suitable courses or training. Ask your local library who to contact.

The **Council for Voluntary Service**, **Council for Social Service** or **Rural Community Council** should be able to help if you want to get involved in voluntary work or community action. They will also have information about groups you can join.

Ask at the **jobcentre** for information about retraining, setting up small businesses, special training opportunities for women and training for unemployed people.

10 Close relationships

'It is easier to be intimate with somebody if you are basically happy about living on your own with your children. You have to learn to care about yourself first.'

'People I am intimate with are people I allow to see the worst in me — but who try to see the best!'

This chapter helps you to look at what you want from the important relationships in your life. It focuses on the good sides of relationships rather than the bad ones. Many lone parents do not need reminding about the bad experiences they have had; they need to regain the confidence that they can have good relationships and trust people.

The chapter also focuses on the people with whom you may have, or have had, a long-term relationship. If you are not in a long-term relationship, or if you do not see this as possible or desirable, you can still use it to help you work out what you would like for the future, or to review past relationships.

How do you feel about intimacy?

Read the statements in the next column and tick any that are close to the way you feel.

There is no 'right or wrong' about these points of view. Most people will feel all of them at some time. Your replies will be influenced by the values held by your family, religion and culture. But they will also depend on your own experience of relationships to date. For example, women who have experienced domestic violence or sexual abuse will have very different feelings from someone whose partner has died or from a lone parent who has chosen to have a child alone.

The statements on the next page may give you some fresh ideas about relationships.

How I feel about intimacy

❏ I love having close relationships.

❏ You can only be really close with one person at a time.

❏ I'm really scared of getting close to people.

❏ I seem to fail at close relationships.

❏ I have never regretted a relationship I've had, even ones that have gone wrong.

❏ I'm frightened to trust someone else because I might be disappointed or rejected.

❏ I'm too easily hurt.

❏ Most people don't come up to my standards.

❏ I don't need people close to me; the children are all that matter.

❏ My next relationship will be better.

❏ I'm afraid of another failure.

❏ Never again!

❏ I don't feel whole if I don't have a partner.

■ Trusting yourself and others

Being comfortable with intimacy and valuing relationships, even if they have ended, are signs of maturity and signs that you know and like yourself.

■ Lack of trust

Many people's experience of relationships makes it difficult for them to trust other people deeply. If you can be clear about the kinds of behaviour you will not put up with, and can watch out for warning signals early on, you may be more likely to choose someone trustworthy. But sometimes we are unable to trust others if we do not trust and like ourselves.

■ Fear of failure

You may feel that you do not want to take the risk of another relationship that might go wrong. But you can learn from experience. You can use your previous experience to ensure that some mistakes are not repeated.

It can be easy to hold others responsible for failure when some of the responsibility may lie with you. Equally, it is easy to take responsibility for things that are not your fault. Be clear about what you have learned and use it positively.

■ Fear of being hurt

Strong emotions can be disturbing if you do not understand them. You may be scared of experiencing the feelings that you had when a previous relationship ended. But the experience of other lone parents (and possibly your own experience) shows that these feelings pass with time. Acknowledging these fears, and talking about the way you feel, is one way of making them less of an obstacle to new relationships.

■ Cutting yourself off from people

Some people get involved with another person, and forget their other friends, 'losing' their own identity in the process. In the same way, losing yourself completely in your children is not good for you or for them. We all need a variety of contacts and relationships. No one person can satisfy all our needs.

What do intimate relationships mean?

Below is a list of some things to be gained from intimate relationships with other adults. Beside each one, write down who provides these for you, including yourself. Add your own points to the list.

What I gain from relationships

- Financial support/security
- Shared responsibility
- Intellectual stimulation
- Emotional support
- Shared decision-making
- Company
- Friendship
- Feeling equal
- Exploring sexuality
- Respect
- Trust
- Love
- Sexual satisfaction
- Another parent for children
- Security
- Practical help
-
-
-

Were there any gaps in your list? If so, are these things that you feel you do not need?

If you do need them, where can you get them from? Most of these things can be provided by friends, relatives, support groups and colleagues, as well as by partners.

Three lone parents' lists are given below.

Amina

- Financial support
  'mother-in-law, ex-husband'
- Shared responsibility
  'I manage without'
- Intellectual stimulation
  'friends, groups'
- Emotional support
  'don't get enough '
- Shared decision-making
  'manage without '
- Company
  'daughter, parents, friends'
- Friendship
  'family, friends'
- Feeling equal
  'don't need'
- Exploring sexuality
  'don't need'
- Respect
  'don't need'
- Trust
  'don't need'
- Love
  'daughter '
- Sexual satisfaction
  'don't need '
- Another parent for children
  'don't need '
- Security
  'could have done with more'
- Practical help
  'could have done with more'

'I realised that I rely on myself a lot to satisfy my needs — perhaps too much. I don't need a partner at the moment, but I would like more support with the responsibility of being a parent and having a home. I get a lot of fulfilment from books, music, art and meditation.'

Laurie

- Financial support
  'me, ex-wife'
- Shared responsibility
  'Diane, childminder'
- Intellectual stimulation
  'Diane, Terry'
- Emotional support
  'Diane, Terry'
- Shared decision-making
  'Diane, ex-wife'
- Company
  'Terry, Diane, Gingerbread'
- Friendship
  'Terry, Diane, Gingerbread'
- Respect
  'childminder'
- Love
  'Diane'
- Sexual satisfaction
  'Diane'
- Another parent for children
  'ex-wife'
- Security
  'me'
- Practical help
  'ex-wife, Terry, childminder, Gingerbread'

'Diane, who I have a long-term relationship with, Terry my best friend and Fran the childminder figure a lot. My ex-wife and I get on well. Made me think about respect and security. Feeling equal? I've never thought about it.'

Michaela

- Shared responsibility
  'brother, friends'
- Intellectual stimulation
  'brother, friends, church, children'
- Emotional support
  'friends, lover, brother, work, God'
- Company
  'friends, children'
- Friendship
  'children, friends, lover, work, church'
- Feeling equal
  'friends'
- Exploring sexuality
  'lover'
- Respect
  'brother, children, friends'
- Trust
  'brother, friends'
- Love
  'lover, brother, children, friends'
- Sexual satisfaction
  'lover, me'
- Another parent for children
  'one friend in particular'
- Security
  'lover, me'
- Practical help
  'friends'
- Real conversation
  'friends, brother'
- Personal growth
  'friends'

'Doing this made me realise how many people I have close to me and how lucky I am.'

Both Michaela and Laurie had a number of people who met their particular needs, rather than relying on one or two people. This seems good and healthy, and ensures that if close partnerships break down, the result need not be totally isolating. Amina, on the other hand, did not feel the need for a close relationship, getting her fulfilment in other ways.

The comments below are on some of the areas in the checklist. Many are from lone parents. Use them to help you examine your relationships and your own attitudes to them. There is no magic formula for good relationships. They are available to anyone willing to put time and effort into developing them.

■ Financial support

It is often hard to get financial support from those around you. Sharing a home with others can ease the financial burden. Families can also help. Many of the lone parents we spoke to had received help from their families — either in cash or through having goods bought for them.

Having a partner does not necessarily mean that you will have financial support. Many men and women have to earn enough to support both themselves and their spouses; many men do not share their money, and women who are not earning may feel far from financially secure. No matter how difficult lone parents find it to manage, many value their financial independence and would not wish to lose it. On the other hand, financial security is important for survival and, for many people, anything and anyone that helps to relieve money pressures is welcome.

■ Shared responsibility

Sharing responsibility for children, home decisions and practical tasks is something lone parents often miss a great deal. In our survey, lone parents felt that *having to do everything for myself and make all the decisions myself, all the time'* was one of the biggest problems they faced. At the same time, though, lone parents valued the greater freedom and independence they had gained from having to do things for themselves. On balance, they did not regret being alone. The solution may be to build up a group of people who will share responsibility with you for some areas

so that it does not have to be a partner that provides this.

'I really wanted someone to share the running around with, but when I had a partner he was such a lousy driver I couldn't trust him to drive me and my daughter at all! It helped me to be more realistic.'

■ Emotional support

Love, friendship, companionship and security, as well as respect, trust and equality are very basic to good relationships. Many people in marriages or other long-term relationships do not give each other emotional support. Friends and relatives do not always provide it either. But in a couple-dominated society it is sometimes not acknowledged that lots of people can provide support, not just a partner. It may be asking too much to expect one person to fulfil all our emotional requirements.

Women have traditionally provided emotional support for each other, and are brought up to do this, as well as provide it for men. Sometimes men want to find a woman partner to provide this kind of caring for themselves and their children, because they cannot, or think that they cannot, provide it themselves. It is better that everyone learns caring skills, and learns to value them.

■ Feeling equal

Equality in relationships is also something to value. Because we live in an unequal society, we may have come to accept inequalities like those between men and women, between white people and black, between heterosexuals and lesbians and gay men, between able-bodied and disabled people, and between middle-class and working-class people. All this means that we usually enter into relationships ready to be 'powerful' or 'weak' although we may not do this consciously. We rarely expect an equal relationship.

Many of the lone parents who wrote in to us said that they had learned a great deal about men's and women's roles from being alone. They had all taken on responsibilities and learned skills that were traditionally seen as belonging to the opposite sex. They had learned new things about themselves and who they were.

Women in heterosexual relationships felt they could no longer go back to a situation where they were seen as 'just' a wife, partner or mother; that they would no longer accept a relationship that was unequal.

If you feel you have changed for the better since becoming a lone parent, you may want to think carefully about going into another relationship where traditional sex-role behaviour might be expected. You also need to think about what this would show your children, who may have learned from your example that women can be strong, independent and in control, or that men can show emotions and be caring.

'I'm so used to constantly examining my outlook and attitude, I couldn't accept a man if he didn't have an open mind.'

Gay and lesbian relationships may seem more equal in this respect, although other types of power inequalities can exist, for example, because of class or race. And it is still easy to fall into a traditional relationship where one partner is 'strong' and the other one 'emotional'.

■ Company

At one time or another most people feel lonely. If you are tempted to blame your loneliness on being a lone parent, it may be comforting to know that many people in couples feel acutely lonely.

'I have felt much more loneliness in "wrong" relationships than on my own.'

'It's important to stress the difference between being alone and being lonely. Some people like to be alone more than others, and choose to be alone for some of the time. They are not lonely.'

'I miss someone to share the joys with more than the sorrow. I've learned to handle the problems now but I find there's no-one to give to!'

Even if you feel that you would like another adult to fill those lonely hours, loneliness in itself is unlikely to be a good enough reason for going into a new relationship. Some people rush into new relationships to 'fill the gap' left by an absent partner and, in doing so, they run the risk of moving from one dependent situation to another.

■ Sexual satisfaction

This is important, but is not the only basis for a good relationship. Being a lone parent means you have greater choice in setting your own standards and the timing and pace of your sexual behaviour. You might have periods without sex, but can still have close, loving relationships with people. If you choose to have sex with someone, it can be on your terms. This is particularly important for women, who may have been brought up to fear sex, to be passive, not to say what they want and not to expect satisfaction. Being a lone parent gives you time to sort out what you want. Men, too, can be caught in a stereotype that expects them to seek satisfaction, be dominant and initiate sex, whether they want to or not. They too may need to unlearn old patterns of behaviour, and learn to be more sensitive and caring.

■ Another parent

The lone parents who wrote to us were clear that looking for a new parent for their children was not a good motive for wanting intimate relationships. If it happened naturally, then this was fine, but it should not be expected. Many pointed out that unless the other parent had died, or was unknown, as with pregnancy by donor, their children already had another parent — however distant they were. Many of the children knew this and were very clear about it. Some children saw a great deal of the parent they were not living with, so it was easier for them to see where all the different relationships fitted in.

Living with yourself

Chapter two, *Parenting alone* looks at the ways lone parents have grown to see themselves as strong, complete human beings. Becoming comfortable with yourself and your own company is an essential part of being able to make good relationships with others.

If you are clear about who you are, and the kind of people you wish to spend your time with, you are more likely to choose relationships where you will not be hurt or oppressed.

When best friends can be worst

Several lone parents in our survey mentioned that friends and acquaintances were often trying to 'pair them off'. This tendency to push people towards becoming a couple — the idea that dinner parties have to have even numbers of men and women; that you cannot go to a dance or party without a partner — has to be challenged. Friends need to know that although you are glad to get invitations, you do not want to feel obliged to 'pair up', and probably other people they invite feel the same way.

Giving and getting

Relationships demand time, energy and effort; they do not just happen. They are also two-way. Where they work well, both people are satisfied that, on balance, they are getting as much as they give. For some people this balance may vary a lot at different times. For others, it may not change.

'What's important is that, overall, it feels right and that as a person you feel important, worthwhile, valuable and respected in this relationship.'

If you are involved with someone on an intimate basis, look at the list below. For each item in the list, first tick the box that matches how much you feel you *give* to the relationship (1 is a little, 5 is a lot). Then for the same item, put another tick to show how much you feel you *get* from the person you have chosen (use another colour for these ticks). Add anything we have missed out.

Ideally, each person should get as much out of a relationship as the other. Your pattern of ticks may show that at the moment your relationships are unequal, or one-sided. For example, you may feel that you give lots of emotional support but get little; you may get practical and financial support but give little. This should all balance out if the different areas have equal value. However, earning money is often given higher status than, say, providing companionship and love. But why should you feel indebted to someone if they give you financial support or practical help, when you give a lot to them in other ways?

If, on balance, the relationship makes you feel good about being who you are, rather than bad, then it is okay. But there may be some areas you need to work on with the other person, particularly if you are falling into patterns you wanted to get away from. You may find it useful to show your list to the other person, or to ask them to complete it too.

What I give and get

	1	2	3	4	5		1	2	3	4	5
Financial support/security	☐	☐	☐	☐	☐	Exploring sexuality	☐	☐	☐	☐	☐
Shared responsibility	☐	☐	☐	☐	☐	Respect	☐	☐	☐	☐	☐
Intellectual stimulation	☐	☐	☐	☐	☐	Trust	☐	☐	☐	☐	☐
Emotional support	☐	☐	☐	☐	☐	Love	☐	☐	☐	☐	☐
Shared decision-making	☐	☐	☐	☐	☐	Sexual satisfaction	☐	☐	☐	☐	☐
Company	☐	☐	☐	☐	☐	Another parent	☐	☐	☐	☐	☐
Friendship	☐	☐	☐	☐	☐	Security	☐	☐	☐	☐	☐
Feeling equal	☐	☐	☐	☐	☐	Practical help	☐	☐	☐	☐	☐

11 Children and your close relationships

'I needed a certain amount of privacy and tried to get this by asking friends to have my son for the night, so I could have the night with my boyfriend. I do wish I could be more open with my child, but until I have a serious relationship I will keep this side of my life a closed book.'

'I believe in privacy and time for myself and my lover, but I also believe that children's needs are important. My son and I will have to respect each other.'

'Until I became really serious about someone, I didn't let anyone stay the night while Isaac was home. This was not because I was embarrassed for him to see me intimate with someone. It was because Isaac has always come into my bed first thing in the morning. This is a very intimate time for us that I didn't want to share with anyone else.'

Intimate relationships do not have to include having sex with someone. But sexual relationships do cause many lone parents a great deal of soul-searching and worry in relation to their children. People have very different views about how openly sex should be discussed, and about how much children should know. This chapter presents some different views and raises some questions.

You may have chosen not to have sexual relationships and that is fine. You may be living in bed-and-breakfast or shared accommodation and may not have the energy, time and space to have intimate relationships. In this case, the chapter may not be helpful to you right now, but it may be useful to help you think for the future.

Children's responses to your dates/lovers

In the next column is a list of children's responses to new partners. Tick the ones that come closest to how each of your children has reacted. Add any that we have not included. Children's reactions will obviously depend on their ages and may change over a period of time.

Your child:
- ❑ tells your partner he or she has come to the wrong address
- ❑ runs away and hides or sulks
- ❑ is sullen and very rude to your partner
- ❑ says she or he does not like your partner
- ❑ fakes illness/refuses to go to school
- ❑ becomes very clinging and whining
- ❑ interrogates your partner about his or her intentions
- ❑ keeps disturbing you and demanding attention if your partner stays the night
- ❑ wants your partner's attention and time continually
- ❑ gets attached to your partner too quickly
- ❑ refuses to do what your partner asks, or plays up
- ❑ makes excessive demands on your attention when she or he knows you are going out
- ❑ refuses to go to bed if you are going out
- ❑ won't settle with a babysitter
- ❑ is pleased because you are happy
- ❑ is surprised because he or she 'didn't think you had it in you'
- ❑ loves having other adults around
- ❑ is relieved because you had been such a misery lately
- ❑ is glad because it makes it easier for her or him to be open about relationships.

All of the bad reactions involve making demands for time and attention, whether by being bad tempered, inquisitive, clinging, over-affectionate or unco-operative. On this page, we look at some of the reasons for this behaviour.

Your children's reactions

■ Jealousy

Children may be jealous of the amount of time your new partner is getting, and may demand a lot more attention than usual. They may not like meeting the person: *'It's the assumption that I ought to welcome this stranger that I resented.'* A child may also show jealousy by demanding a lot of attention from your new friend, when you want her/him for yourself.

'She got on well with him when I wasn't there but when we were all together she kept vying for my attention and would declare at regular intervals that she hated him.

'I found it incredibly hard to handle. I really wanted to spend the day with him but couldn't be myself and I certainly wasn't giving Louise her usual ration of care and attention. Dave understood the problem and left after lunch so that Louise and I could salvage the day together. I told her that I thought it must feel strange and be hard for her to see me with someone else I love, and that I thought she must feel jealous and angry at me and it probably made her dislike Dave.

'I hoped that by showing her I understood and accepted her feelings she would at least try and accept mine. She didn't want to talk about it at all and preferred to get back to doing what we normally do. I guess that's fair for a 2 year old.'

■ Insecurity

Children who have lost a parent through death, separation or desertion may worry that they will lose the other one, or that someone else will take their place in their parent's affections.

'They had met him once when he came to take me out, but they were not warned that he would be staying the first night. They walked into the bedroom and said, "Daddy, oh no, Derek, hello!", and promptly jumped all over him — no problem except the next time I was going out they didn't

want me to go. Perhaps they thought "Daddy found someone else and left, and mummy will too!". It took a lot of persuading otherwise.'

'I don't want my dad to marry his girlfriend because if they had a child, I would feel he wouldn't really be my father anymore.'

■ Prejudice and hostility

Children's behaviour often reflects the attitudes and values they see around them. Sometimes these attitudes are different from your own. So, for example, if you have chosen to have a gay or lesbian relationship, or if you are white and have chosen a black partner, you may have to deal with the negative attitudes about homosexuality or about black people transmitted to your children by our society.

■ Conflicts of loyalty

Children may worry that they will be expected to treat a new partner as if he or she were their other parent. If they still have a relationship with the absent parent, they can feel awkward about this, and pulled in different directions. Or, if their other parent has died, they may feel you are being 'disloyal' in starting a new relationship. This unease may show itself through the children asking too many questions, being rude to the person or refusing to relate to her or him.

'I hope mum never gets remarried because I just wouldn't like anyone else to try and take the place of dad.'

■ Disappointment

Children may want more from your partners than they can have. For example, they may expect that people will pay them attention or include them in everything. They may get attached to your partners, and be disappointed if things do not work out.

'With my first boyfriend we spoke of marriage to both our families and my son couldn't understand when things didn't work out. With the second, the first thing he asked was whether we were going to marry. When I said "no", he wanted to know why not. He was very upset the first time. I do not want to hurt him again. Until I'm sure, no man will stay with me while my son is here.'

Your feelings

■ Your unease

If you feel uneasy about having your own relationships, you may make a big thing out of leaving the children with, say, a babysitter. If you feel you cannot leave until they are settled, they may pick this up, and refuse to settle, with the result that you get more uneasy or even resentful. Some lone parents decide they are uneasy because they feel guilty.

'If children are old enough, they shouldn't be pushed to bed, but should understand that you must have your evenings and nights to yourself.'

You may also genuinely feel pulled in different directions. You want to care for and please everyone, and divide your attention fairly. But adults and children may sense your confusion and exploit this. You do not want to be put in a position of having to choose between your children and adult relationships.

■ Your uncertainties

You may not feel uneasy or guilty about the relationship, but you may not be clear about where it is going. Children can pick up your uncertainty and use it to their advantage:

'I'm confused about my steady relationship: I don't know what I want. I think this rubs off on my daughter and she senses that if she moans and grumbles and gently persuades me not to go to my boyfriend's she wins just to make life easier.'

■ Your reactions

It is difficult to ignore children's behaviour. If you try, it can often create more stress. So you need to deal with the behaviour, and also the reasons behind it. Any of the following reactions is quite natural:

- feeling guilty
- getting angry with your children
- resenting them for limiting your activities
- insisting on your rights
- talking to them honestly about their behaviour
- giving in and not having relationships, even though you would like to
- deciding not to have lovers for the moment
- hiding your relationships.

What can you do?

Guilt is a common feeling. If you have been brought up to feel that 'marriage is forever', but your own marriage has ended, you may feel bad about having relationships even though you know there is no reason to feel guilty. You need to believe that any relationships you have are for the best. As one lone parent summed up:

'Because I am free from guilt, the children can't complain. My happiness affects theirs.'

Anger and resentment can be destructive reactions. You need to understand your children's feelings and to help them respect your right to have relationships. If you feel angry, you may not pay enough attention to how your children are feeling.

You also need to be realistic about the changes that having children has made to your life. You cannot have relationships in the same way as you did before you had children. There are things you can no longer easily do on the spur of the moment, like staying out all night, making love, coming home late or going out for a meal. You swopped this kind of freedom for the pleasure of having children. Planning ahead and keeping your children informed of your plans is essential. Somehow you need to find a balance between your responsibilities to your children and your own rights as an individual.

Children need firm reassurance that they will not lose you (or their other parent, if he or she is around). They need to feel included in any new adult relationship, with clear limits which they can understand.

They need to be cuddled, especially if the other adult receives such affection in front of them. They need to know that they are still loved and as important as they were before.

'I include my child in a kiss and cuddle, recognising that he's feeling left out.'

Be responsible, for example, by coming home when you say you will and by keeping children informed about any changes to your plans.

'Tell the children you have a date and are going out. Answer questions and if children want to meet your date, let them.'

'Be as consistent as is humanly possible. I am a great believer in being honest (in a way children can understand), allowing my children time alone with me and being able to let them see that I am human.'

▇ Asserting your rights

Children need to understand that you are entitled to your own friends and interests, and that this does not mean you love them any less.

'I say that she has her friends and she would not like it if I didn't let her see them. I say that I'm entitled to fun just like she is. I think she understands.'

'I decided I would not let my children rule me. If I wanted to have a man friend, I would. I stated this clearly, emphasising that I would always love them and be here, and that no man would take me away from them. This they accepted.'

'I tell them they must share me and I'm not theirs alone.'

▇ Not having relationships

You may choose to avoid new relationships altogether, either in response to your children's behaviour or for other reasons. Quite a few lone parents who wrote to us had decided to put off having a serious relationship until the children were grown up. If you are happy with this, fine, but if you resent it, nobody will be happy.

Handling your children's difficult behaviour: some good advice

- Talk to the children about their behaviour soon after the event.

- Help the children put their feelings into words: 'You seem ... ', or 'I wonder if you act like that because ... ', could be ways of bringing up the subject.

- Understand the children's feelings or recognise where these feelings have come from (as, for example, in the case of racist behaviour).

- Ask about their behaviour and praise them when they give you an honest answer. For example, 'I'm afraid there won't be any love for me'; 'I don't think it's right for men to go out with men'; 'I can't stand that person ...'

- Deal with any fears, anxieties, or prejudices by providing accurate information.

- Discuss how your children's behaviour affects others. Help them to understand that the behaviour is not good for them, and can hurt adults.

- Reach an agreement on changing their behaviour by a specific time; do not ask for complete change immediately, take it a step at a time.

- Notice when the children do improve their behaviour, and praise them for it.

■ Partners and parents replaced

Partners and 'dates' are not children's parents and should not act as though they are, at least not without everyone's agreement. You should make it clear that a lover is not taking the place of the other parent, nor is the new partner taking the child's place in your love. Avoid talking about your partner in terms of 'maybe this will be a new mummy or daddy'. If you are unsure or uneasy about this, the children will pick it up.

Talking to the absent parent, as well as the new partner, will help. You can then ask for support in reassuring the children. You may need to review your own ideas about intimate relationships, your reasons for wanting them and the role they play in your life. Read the chapter *Close relationships* on page 73.

■ Respecting your children's privacy

Your children need to learn to respect your right to have friends, privacy and time away from them. They, too, need to have their privacy respected. You can have rules in your home which your partners or dates have to keep -- for example, what time they have to leave the home; how freely can they move around the house; which rooms they can go into, and so on. Children should not feel their home is being taken over without their agreement.

And if your children cannot stand your particular choice of relationship, or if your new partner does not respect your children's rights, is he or she really right for you?

'If someone I liked didn't get on with the children, I suppose I would take that into account and not start anything with him', wrote one of the parents we contacted.

Your children and your sex life

'Being young, the children adapt very easily, but where do I draw the moral line? It's not a problem in marriage, but what is a socially acceptable single sex life? None at all? Not in front of the children? Only with one regular partner? Hell, I don't know, so how can I teach them? This I find is one of the biggest problems.'

These words, written by one of the lone parents we contacted, must sum up the situation for lots of people. Whether or not you have been married, there is still a view that where children are involved, relationships between people who are not married, or are not living together on a permanent basis, are seen as odd and often immoral. Relationships with members of the same sex are definitely seen as deviant. Gay and lesbian parents rarely get custody of their children anyway as it is seen as an 'abnormal' situation in which to raise children. Section 28 of the 1988 Local Government Act even describes their relationships as 'pretended family relationships'.

There is no agreement as to what is the 'right' way to behave sexually. Religious, cultural and other values guide our views and behaviour. Society sets standards that make it more acceptable for men to be sexually active than women, although this is changing slowly. Words like 'promiscuous', 'easy' and 'loose' are almost exclusively insults to women, not men. Double standards exist, and sexual freedom is much more acceptable for men than for women.

Families also differ a great deal in their attitudes towards nakedness, how much parents and children of different ages touch and cuddle, and whether children are able to join their parents in bed during the night or early in the morning.

It is likely that you will either follow standards set by others, or that you will have worked out a set of principles that feel comfortable for you. Good guiding principles are that you do not hurt, oppress or exploit others.

People usually want their children to behave the same way they do. You cannot set rules for your children that are different from the ones you practise yourself. If you feel uncomfortable with your own behaviour, this discomfort will be passed on to your children. The questionnaire which follows should help you identify what is wrong and right for you, and work out how to convey this to your children.

Sexual relationships and your children

Below are a number of statements describing how lone parents might feel about their sexual relationships. Tick the ones that come closest to your views.

■ Overall

❑ I never have people to stay the night and I keep my sex life totally private.

❑ I only have someone to stay the night if we are in a serious relationship.

❑ I quite freely have people to stay the night at any time and my children are around as they please.

❑ I don't agree with sex outside marriage.

❑ I don't have sexual partners at all.

■ About your children seeing you in bed with another adult

❑ I know it's my right but I still feel strange about it.

❑ My partner always leaves before the children wake up.

❑ I feel fine about having partners to stay.

❑ I just wouldn't have someone to stay at all.

❑ My partner has to pretend she or he has come round for breakfast.

■ How much do your children know?

❑ Everything they want to — I don't make a big thing about it, but answer their questions.

❑ I always let them know in advance, when someone is coming to stay the night.

❑ I have my sex life elsewhere — they know I am staying with someone.

❑ They don't know anything — but I think they must guess.

❑ They meet everyone I am close to.

❑ They don't know.

■ Your privacy

❑ The children come into bed whenever they want in the middle of the night or early in the morning.

❑ If someone's with me, I lock the door.

❑ They know they have to knock if the bedroom door is closed.

❑ My children sleep in the same room as me and they have to stay elsewhere if I want anyone to sleep at home.

❑ I can only get privacy if I stay elsewhere without the children.

■ Your fears

❑ That the children will be disturbed by seeing a stranger in bed with me.

❑ That my behaviour is morally wrong.

❑ That I will lose my children's respect.

❑ That my behaviour will make them become irresponsible, promiscuous teenagers or adults.

❑ That the children will resent the new person for seeming to take their other parent's place.

❑ That the children will 'tell' the other parent.

❑ That my family/community will disapprove because they feel it will damage the children.

Your pattern of answers may fall into one or more groups:

■ An open approach
'Sleeping with people is part of a close relationship, so it would be silly to let the children think otherwise.'

An open approach acknowledges that lone parents, like others, have a right to have sexual relationships with other adults, and that children need to accept that this is part of who their parents are. It allows children to see that sex is a part of loving someone (although loving someone does not have to include sex). Sex is not a secret, and if the children see the partner around the home it means that they will not fantasise about what *'mummy or daddy do when away from me'* and *'what goes on when children are in bed'*.

One of the advantages of an open approach is that children see that their parent is loved and therefore worthy of love. However, you need to be comfortable with your own sexuality for it to work this way, otherwise the children will pick up your discomfort.

Being open does not mean you have to tell children all the details of your sex life, let them see you having sex, or have long discussions with them about it. It just means that you answer their questions as truthfully as possible and that you do not keep your relationships secret or furtive. Simple explanations can be sufficient.

For example:

'I sometimes want a friend to stay the night, just like you do' or *'I need another adult around sometimes'*.

■ If you do not want to be completely open
'I'm dating four people at the same time and sleeping with two of them. As none of them is really important to me yet, I don't want my children to see them coming or going. I believe there's a place for discretion in one's sex life and this is definitely it. I also think I'm entitled to some privacy.'

If you do not want to keep your relationships completely secret, but have strong views about how and when your children should get to know a new partner, you need to work out where you will draw the line. For example, you may decide that you will only introduce your partners to your children if and when the relationship becomes a long-term one. But if you have been going out with someone for a while and have not allowed the children to see you in bed together, what will it mean to the children when this does happen?

Some suggestions for helping this approach to work:

● Try and arrange for the children to be absent on the first few nights that you sleep with someone. This gives you a chance to get comfortable with the relationship yourself before involving the children.

● If you decide to spend the night away, plan ahead. Make sure you have a reliable babysitter, friend or relative to stay, and leave an emergency telephone number, either of where you will be, or of a trusted person they can phone if necessary.

■ A closed approach
You may feel you want to keep your sexual relationships completely private from your children; that they are none of the children's business. You do not need to make sex a secret, just not talk about it openly unless children ask.

If you do find it difficult to talk about sex, and feel it is something that children should not know about because they are too young or you just do not want them involved, think about how you would answer children's questions like:

'Why can't we come with you?'
'Who is Aisha / Frank / Jo who keeps phoning?'
'Where are you going?'
'Where do you go when you stay away every Tuesday night?'

If you are doing something you do not agree with — which is why you do not want the children to know about it — isn't this hypocritical? If you do not practise what you preach, what kind of model are you providing for teenage children who may be exploring their own sexuality?

■ Being open, but private

Establishing privacy for yourself is very important, whether or not you intend to have sexual partners. Your children have to learn that you need time for yourself, time without them and time with others.

In return, they too need their privacy. If you want them to knock on your door, you also have to knock on theirs. If you want private time, they should have it too.

- Even small children can learn that grown-ups have areas of personal privacy. For example, closing a bathroom door, not necessarily for modesty, teaches children that doors are closed sometimes and do not get opened until the person in the bathroom chooses.

- You can make the bedroom 'out of bounds', except by invitation, and go there for 'your time'. You may need to lock it until the children have learned to knock and not just barge in. You can put up funny 'Do not disturb' signs so it becomes serious but light-hearted.

Children's attachments

'I always encouraged Isaac to get close to several of my adult friends so that a 'failed' relationship of mine would have less of an impact on him.'

If you have been in a close, long-term relationship with another adult, your children will be fond of the partner. If the relationship then breaks up, the children are likely to grieve and miss the partner. Their feelings need to be taken into account; they need to know where they stand, what is happening and whether there are any implications for them. They also need time to adjust to the changes. The chapter *Your children's feelings* (page 31) can help here.

The majority of lone parents probably have straightforward relationships. Many stand back and allow their children and their lovers to develop their own friendships.

Three lone parents describe what has worked for them:

Sheila

'They've seen people I've slept with at breakfast and I think that because I don't make a great thing of it, they've just accepted it as they would if they had a friend to stay. They've always known the person in question before this happens. I make a point of inviting the person to meet the children several times before staying the night. I give the children a lot of independence, and I think that's why they appreciate that I must have mine too. They've never asked when is so-and-so going to be their new parent. I'm sure because it's never entered my head, it's never entered theirs.'

Bryony

'My children have been aware of two long-term relationships in which I have been involved. On each occasion the children have been allowed to get to know my partner and have always known that he would be staying overnight before this happened, rather than afterwards. Unfortunately, when I decided to end the first of these relationships, the children were very distressed. This obviously upset me and when they realised this and we talked about it they became extremely supportive. I am fortunate that neither partner ever tried to become the "heavy father" and my children always got on well with them.'

Shola

'About five months ago I met another man — this is my first proper relationship since my marriage broke up. I keep Simon quite apart from the children, they often meet him but only for about five minutes before going to bed, or he might pop in for half an hour here and there, but he isn't trying to take over their lives. It's all happening gradually and they are used to him being my boyfriend. I have had no adverse behaviour, they like him (and his car) and he likes them. He does not interfere with their lives or their time with me, so he is not a big secret or threat, but at the same time he is not taking over their father's role.

'At present it is working out very well. They ask all the usual questions — "Do you love him?" "Does he love you?" "Will you marry him?" and so on. The only answer I can give is that at the moment I don't wish to live with him or marry him, but I might want to eventually — which satisfies them. There appears to be no jealousy or fears. I have not encouraged Simon to spend days with us as a family and most definitely he does not stay over night, as I do not know what the future holds for us, and I don't want the boys becoming too attached to him or dependent on him. Only time will tell, but I feel happy with the situation at present.'

12 Meeting other lone parents

'There are so many lone parents and we need lone parent groups to get to know each other. I feel less isolated and I'm also happier on my daughter's behalf because she meets other kids in her position and I'm sure she feels more "normal" because of it.'

Lone parents can offer each other many things. This chapter looks at some of them.

How do you feel about meeting other lone parents? These are some lone parents' views: tick any that you agree with, or add your own.

How do you feel?

❑ I have little in common with other lone parents.
❑ I don't think anyone needs to know that I'm a lone parent.
❑ I don't go out of my way to meet other lone parents, but it's surprising how many I come into contact with while doing other things.
❑ I have enough friends of my own, and I'm not looking for any more.
❑ My closest friends are lone parents too.
❑ I wish I could meet other lone parents – where are they?
❑
❑
❑

Your feelings about meeting other lone parents will depend on a number of things. You may already have a lot of support from friends and family. Or you may wish to 'play down' being a lone parent because you have been affected by the widespread prejudice against lone parents. On the other hand, you may have discovered the value of having lone parents as friends. Your attitude will also depend on how easy you find it to meet people in other ways, for example at work, as a member of a tenants' association, or through your children.

What can lone parents offer each other?

Comments from the lone parents who took part in our survey fell into four main areas:

● knowledge and information about financial, legal, practical and other aspects of being a lone parent

● friendship, understanding and support for each other

● practical help with and sharing of the responsibilities of being a parent

● positive role-models for children, showing lone parents as competent and strong, in contrast to the stereotypes which depict one parent families as 'deprived' or 'from broken homes'.

Of course, it is not only lone parents who can offer these things. But support from other lone parents is especially valuable because of the experiences they have in common.

The questionnaire on the next page will help you work out what you have to offer others, and what you want from them. Obviously you can also get these things from people who are not lone parents. And you do not always need other people to help you do these things. But even if you do not want to rely on other lone parents too often, it is good to know they are there if you need them.

What I need from other lone parents, and what I have to offer

Read through the list below and put a tick in the first column beside each kind of support you would like from other lone parents. In the second column, tick what you can offer other lone parents. This exercise may help you recognise your strengths, particularly if you feel you have not got much to offer. There is space at the end for you to add ideas of your own.

	What I want	What I can give
• A listening ear.	☐	☐
• Someone who understands what it's like.	☐	☐
• Someone in a similar situation to me.	☐	☐
• Someone who cares about me.	☐	☐
• Someone who makes me feel 'normal'.	☐	☐
• A friend.	☐	☐
• Someone to help give me confidence.	☐	☐
• Someone who will encourage me.	☐	☐
• Someone who will take what I have to offer.	☐	☐
• Someone to go out and do things with.	☐	☐
• Someone to babysit.	☐	☐
• Someone to help with daytime childcare.	☐	☐
• Someone who will accept my children and help them feel positive about being in a one parent family.	☐	☐
• Someone to go shopping with.	☐	☐
• Someone to help with tasks in the house.	☐	☐
• Someone to share meals with.	☐	☐
• Someone to call on in an emergency.	☐	☐
• Someone to help me know my rights.	☐	☐
• Someone to help with finances.	☐	☐
• Someone to tell me what's going on locally.	☐	☐
• Someone to have fun with.	☐	☐
• Someone who can speak my language and understands my cultural background.	☐	☐
•	☐	☐
•	☐	☐
•	☐	☐

How to meet other lone parents

'Once I told people at work that I was a lone parent, I found that several others were too.'

'I hated the thought of going to the parent and toddler group because I thought I'd be the only lone parent. My friend had to nearly drag me there. But the group organiser was really nice, and introduced me to three other lone parents.'

'I talked to my children's teachers at school about the changes that the children will have to cope with now that I am a lone parent. The teachers each said that there were a number of other children from one parent families in their classes, and introduced me to them. I made four good friends because of this.'

'I saw notices in the library advertising two local groups for lone parents.'

'I advertised in the local paper for other lone fathers. I got three replies and we have started to meet regularly on Sunday mornings.'

'I joined the tenants' association when our flats were in danger of being sold to a private company. It was amazing how many other people on the estate were bringing up children on their own.'

Some suggestions:

- Join activities not specially for lone parents. You may be surprised how many you find.
- Advertise in libraries, community centres, and local papers for other lone parents to contact you. But think about whether you want your address and phone number available to anyone. You may prefer to use a box number.
- Look out for groups or individuals who might advertise for new members or contacts.
- National magazines often take adverts or have a 'pen-pals', 'lonely hearts' or groups' page.
- *Ginger*, Gingerbread's newspaper, has a contacts column. It can also put you in touch with a local group; there may be lone parents living nearby who you do not know.
- Just letting people know you are a lone parent may lead to other people contacting you.

Lone parents in groups

What do you think about groups for lone parents?

'At first I felt I couldn't join a group. I couldn't face other lone parents or deal with the fact that I am one. Now I feel that groups provide a wonderful outlet for lone parents so that they don't feel alone.'

'I had a few bad experiences at first with some groups, especially those run by men. However, I now help run a Gingerbread group which fulfils a personal and emotional need for me.'

'My first thought was "No, it's not for me — I'm not that type". Then I saw an article in the local newspaper about someone wanting to start a group. That did interest me. I think the idea of walking into an established group scared me, whereas, by starting from scratch, there would be plenty for me to do so I wouldn't think about myself.'

These three lone parents had different experiences, but all had found ways of getting something useful from groups despite their initial reservations.

The people we surveyed saw the main benefits of lone parent groups as:

- meeting others in the same situation
- sharing and supporting
- good experiences for the children
- a positive identity for lone parenting
- building confidence
- reducing isolation
- a new social life
- outings and events with the children.

In addition, groups often provide:

- advice and information
- an opportunity to take part in social or political activities, community action or group discussions
- the chance to share your hobbies and enjoy them with others who feel the same as you do
- the opportunity to learn new skills
- the opportunity to grow and change as a person, and to play a part in other people's change and growth too.

Groups you could join

Gingerbread has a network of 300 local groups that meet regularly. They always welcome new members.

Gingerbread groups organise family events and outings for parents and children. They offer the chance for lone parents to get involved in new activities and interests. Most have regular weekly or fortnightly meetings where children are welcome. Other groups may not include children, but some lone parents prefer this and can make suitable arrangements.

Local libraries usually have a list of all clubs, groups and societies in your area. Health centres, library notice boards, the local Council for Voluntary Service, community centres and Citizens Advice Bureaux also display information on groups.

Groups often publicise the name and telephone number of someone who you can contact. You can ask them any questions about the group and get an impression of how welcoming the group will be.

Anxieties about joining groups

It takes courage and confidence to go into a group, particularly if you do not know anyone there. Many people feel anxious about joining groups and it can help to know that you are not the only one with these feelings.

Some of the lone parents who wrote to us had reservations about joining groups. We have listed their comments below, plus our suggestions for ways of overcoming the reservations.

'I was nervous at first. I didn't want to be labelled. I persevered and made new friends.' Going along even if you do not feel like it can help you realise that in many ways the people you are worried about meeting are no different from yourself.

'They can be clique-ish — difficult to get into.' Ask how they introduce new members and whether there are members who live nearby who you could meet beforehand.

'My initial approach to a group was difficult. I was wary and unsure that black people would be welcomed.' Ask if there are any other black people in the group; see if some members of the group will meet you beforehand; take a friend along with you.

'You can't choose group members like you choose friends.' True, but you can make new friends from group members.

'When you first go you really feel like an outsider.' This is a very common feeling but you can make it easier by getting to know someone from the group beforehand, or going along with a friend.

'Groups are fine as long as everyone is treated equally.' Gingerbread has a policy on equality that its groups should be putting into practice.

'As a woman with a disability, I can't easily attend group meetings and I have yet to find a group where I don't have to make an effort all the time.' Gingerbread's equal opportunities policy covers disability; groups should be aware of how to make disabled people welcome, and how to provide the facilities they need.

One lone parent who wrote to us summed up the value of groups:

'In my Gingerbread group everyone knows that they have something to offer and that what they have to offer is valued. They also know the group won't work without all of us so we all pull together and do our bit to keep the group going. There's lots of give and take.'

Contacts

Exploring Parenthood runs workshops for parents. Ring London (071) 607 9647.

Parent Network is a national network helping to improve relationships between parents and children. Ring London (071) 485 8535.

Gingerbread provides support, help and social activities for lone parents and their children via a national network of mutual aid groups. For information about local groups, ring London (071) 240 0953.

Getting better all the time

This book ends, as it began, with the voices of lone parents. All of the quotations on this page come from parents who were involved in writing this book. These everyday success stories show how being a lone parent can be a rewarding and liberating experience.

'I have been an active Gingerbread member for the last five years. Gingerbread helped me tremendously with friendship, empathy, support and a better social life. For the past two years I have been trying to better my education. To date I have an 'O' level for Accounts and Bookkeeping and a GCSE in English, and I am sitting further exams this year. The last few years have been painful and hard work, but I am a better person. I am stronger, more determined and I have the confidence to do anything!'

'I am 48 years old. I had my only child at 44 having spent a lifetime ensuring I didn't become a parent. Regardless of the problems of being a lone parent I feel happy to have my son.'

'I was shattered, unemployed, penniless and nearly lost our home. I got a job and some retraining, and five years ago deliberately got pregnant and had a third son. We are a happy family. We recently spent a year in the USA on an exchange. Lone parenting is great. Husbands are a waste of time!'

'Four years ago I was lost in my emotions (mostly self-pity) and my world was shattered when I was left for the "younger woman". It's taken me a long time, but now, with the help of my friends, I feel happy to be an independent person and parent who can make my own decisions.'

'I'm independent, liberated and generally happy about the way I handle single parenthood. I'm going to college to do teacher training in September and I'm looking forward to the mental stimulation and the adult company — but I dread leaving my daughter at the nursery all day because she's the best thing ever!'

'I've learnt a new respect for myself — that I do not need a man in my life to feel fulfilled. I can do anything I want to. I've also learnt to look at myself, to be honest about my capabilities in terms of what I can give to others.'

'I'm totally independent now — no-one to criticise what I do or attempt to do. I am taking a college course in Community Care / Home Nursing and hope to get a City and Guilds at the end of it.'

'I came from a "difficult" background, and became pregnant — after meningitis "they" thought he was unadoptable. I've discovered I'm powerful and strong. I know now I have amazing potential and I will use it to great benefit soon. I'm glad it all happened — have a wonderful son and enjoy our relationship.'

'I was always very shy and nervous, but since I have been on my own I have been forced out of that situation because of having to do everything myself and make all the decisions. It has really boosted my confidence. I realise now it was the best thing I could have done as my son is so much happier and more settled, and so am I. Also I have learned to do so many things for myself that I never bothered to do before.'